A GUIDE TO HAWAI'I'S
COASTAL
PLANTS

Other Books by Michael Walther

Images of Natural Hawai'i: A Pictorial Guide of the Aloha State's Native Forest Birds and Plants

Pearls of Pearl Harbor

A Guide to

Hawai'i's
Coastal
Plants

Michael Walther

MUTUAL PUBLISHING

DEDICATION

For my dear Cecilia

All photos copyright© by Michael Walther.

Design by wanni

Library of Congress Catalog Card Number: 2004102116
ISBN 1-56647-653-4

First Printing, May 2004
Second Printing, May 2017

Mutual Publishing, LLC
1215 Center Street, Suite 210
Honolulu, Hawai'i 96816
Ph: (808) 732-1709 Fax: (808) 734-4094
info@mutualpublishing.com
www.mutualpublishing.com
Printed in South Korea

TABLE OF CONTENTS

Heliotropium anomalum
Heliotropium curassavicum
Heteropogon contortus
Ipomoea pes-caprae
Jacquemontia ovalifolia
Lepidium bidentatum
Lipochaeta integrifolia
Lipochaeta lobata
Lycium sandwicense
Lysimachia mauritiana
Marsilea villosa
Metrosideros polymorpha
Myoporum sandwicense
Nama sandwicensis
Nototrichium sandwicense
Osteomeles anthyllidifolia
Pandanus tectorius
Plectranthus parviflorus
Plumbago zeylanica
Portulaca lutea
Portulaca molokiniensis
Portulaca villosa
Pseudognaphalium sandwicensium
Psydrax odorata
Reynoldsia sandwicensis
Santalum ellipticum
Scaevola coriacea
Scaevola taccada
Schiedea adamantis
Schiedea globosa
Senna gaudichaudii
Sesbania tomentosa
Sesuvium portulacastrum
Sida fallax
Solanum nelsonii
Sporobolus virginicus
Tetramolopium rockii
Tribulus cistoides
Vigna marina
Vitex rotundifolia
Waltheria indica
Wikstroemia uva-ursi

ACKNOWLEDGMENTS

I thank professional botanists Robert Hobdy, Clyde Imada and David Lorence for kindly assisting in the Hawaiian plant species identification and to Sam Gon and Forrest Starr for information regarding locations of native Hawaiian coastal plants. Thanks to Tina Barnes and Tamara Sherrill Nelson of Maui Nui Botanical Gardens for assistance with photographing several rare species; Allison Wright for sharing her knowledge of plants found at Maui's Wailea Point Native Plant Seawalk and Matt Schirman of Hui Kū Maoli Ola, a native plant nursery located in Waimānalo, Oʻahu. Thanks also to Dr. Sherwin Carlquist for teaching Island Biology. His entertaining lectures on Hawaiian natural history, illustrated with an excellent array of slides, posters, and hands-on examples inspired me to pursue a greater understanding and association with Hawaiʻi's native bird and plant species. I also thank Bennett Hymer and the staff of Mutual Publishing for their interest and assistance with this guide. Thanks to my brother Mark, for his great generosity and kindness.

Special thanks to my dear wife and soul mate, Cecilia, for her boundless love, friendship and inspiration; and for her many great contributions toward our mutual goals of exploring Hawaiʻi's diverse ecosystem, photographing unique native species and publicizing the urgent need to save what remains.

M y goal in writing this book was to create an easy-to-use field guide that would assist in identifying many of the plant species that you might encounter while exploring Hawai'i's shoreline and coastal areas. Several books have been written about Hawaiian coastal plants, but I wanted to write one that would include more native species in order to present a better idea of the spectacular diversity that exists and to provide information about the best remaining locations where you can go to observe some of the finest examples of intact native Hawaiian coastal plant ecosystems. This guide is intended for the lay person and does not include detailed, scientific botanical descriptions. I would highly recommend the excellent and comprehensive *Manual of the Flowering Plants of Hawai'i* for the serious botanical student.

The Hawaiian coastal vegetation zone has been defined differently by various authors. In this guide, I have included plant species found from sea level to 1,000-feet elevation. In *Plants and Flowers of Hawai'i*, Sohmer and Gustafson list the following zones found completely or partially below 1,000-feet elevation: strand (coastal sites affected by salt spray), coastal (not influenced by salt spray or seawater) and dryland forest and shrub. This guide contains many, but not all, native Hawaiian plant species from these three zones.

My hope is that by learning about, locating and identifying native Hawaiian coastal plants, which represent products of spectacular evolution over countless centuries, you will be charmed by their great beauty and uniqueness and saddened by their awful fate. Maybe you, too, will be inspired to participate in conservation efforts toward their continued existence. The surviving native species barely exist in scattered remnants of once beautiful and thriving ecosystems. They represent a priceless, irreplaceable part of Hawai'i's magnificent natural treasure. Living on the most valuable and accessible Hawaiian land has contributed to their terrible decline. Perhaps by working together, we can preserve some of those few native Hawaiian coastal plants that remain.

Michael Walther
Honolulu, Hawai'i
2004

INTRODUCTION

M ore than 80,000,000 years ago, in a spot close to the center of the Pacific Ocean, fiery volcanic explosions turned the salt water into a boiling, steamy cauldron. Violent bursts of lava were ejected above the ocean's surface and an island began to form. Fed by 2,000-degree magma rising from deep within the Earth's mantle, the new volcano continued to grow. Hundreds of thousands of years passed as this remote island gained land area. It might have eventually reached a height of 10,000-feet or more above the barren windswept sea. This was Meiji, the oldest of more than 80 volcanoes that today are known as the Hawaiian Ridge and Emperor Seamount Chain. Each of these volcanoes shares a common volcanic origin and was created over a semi-stationary plume of lava called the Hawaiian hot spot. One of the world's great tectonic plates, the Pacific plate, has slowly carried the volcanic islands away from the hot spot at a rate of 3 1/2-inches per year toward the north, shifting to the northwest 43,000,000 years ago. Like a gigantic conveyor belt, the volcanoes were formed and carried away.

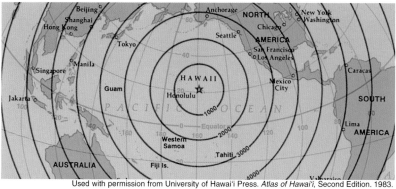

Used with permission from University of Hawai'i Press. *Atlas of Hawai'i*, Second Edition. 1983.

As one moved away from the hot spot, another was formed behind it. The Hawaiian Ridge Emperor and Seamount Chain stretches more than 3,800-miles from one end to the other. Today, Meiji is located off the coast of Siberia's Kamchatka Peninsula and is 3,000-feet below sea level. Kure Atoll, the northernmost of the Hawaiian Islands and the northernmost coral atoll in the world, is approximately 27,000,000-years old and is located over 1,600-miles north of Honolulu. The oldest of the eight main islands is Kaua'i, with an estimated age of 5,000,000 years.

The Hawaiian Islands are the most isolated group of large islands in the world and one of the remotest places on Earth. The west coast of North America, the closest continent to the Hawaiian chain, is 2,400-miles away. Japan is 3,800-miles to the west, and our nearest group of high-island neighbors, the Marquesas, is over 2,000-miles to the southeast.

After the flows of the ancient volcanoes had sufficiently cooled, tiny spores of colonizing algae, moss, lichen and fungus species that arrived could now survive on the warm, black, porous lava rock. Swept aloft to great altitudes and transported thousands of

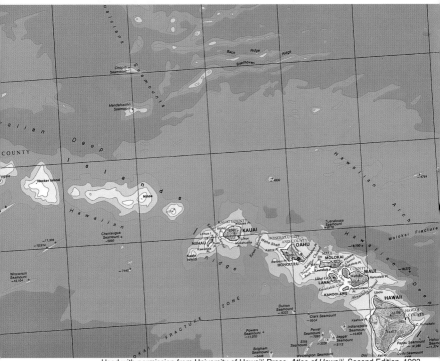

Used with permission from University of Hawai'i Press. *Atlas of Hawai'i*, Second Edition. 1983.

miles by strong air currents, the nearly frozen minute propagules of these primitive plant groups survived a miraculous crossing to become the first organisms to successfully reach the sterile, isolated volcanic outposts. If you place 1,000 of these dust-like spores end to end, the line would only measure an inch long!

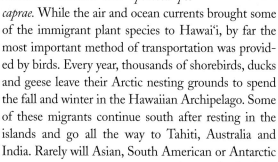

Seeds were also carried to the isolated volcanic islands of Hawai'i by ocean currents. Some examples of plant seeds that arrived by seawater flotation include *Erythrina sandwicensis, Pandanus tectorius* and *Ipomoea pes-caprae.* While the air and ocean currents brought some of the immigrant plant species to Hawai'i, by far the most important method of transportation was provided by birds. Every year, thousands of shorebirds, ducks and geese leave their Arctic nesting grounds to spend the fall and winter in the Hawaiian Archipelago. Some of these migrants continue south after resting in the islands and go all the way to Tahiti, Australia and India. Rarely will Asian, South American or Antarctic

species wander far from their usual migration paths and show up lost in Hawai'i. Some of the birds are carrying seeds from distant shores. The seeds are either embedded in the mud on the bird's feet, stuck to its feathers by a glue-like substance or barbed hook or inside the bird's digestive tract.

Carlquist examined many native Hawaiian plant species' seeds to determine their method of dispersal. He calculated that 1.4 % of the 270 successful original immigrant plant species, from which all of Hawai'i's current 1,060 native Hawaiian plants evolved, arrived by air, 22.8% reached Hawai'i by sea and the remaining 75.8% were brought by birds. Fosberg concluded that 18% of the successful colonizing plant species came from the Americas, 17% from Australia, 3% from the Arctic and the greatest number, 40%, had Indo-Pacific origins. Twelve percent were thought to be cosmopolitan and not from any particular area and the remaining 10% was uncertain.

The chances of a plant species successfully dispersing its seed, to Hawai'i was extremely low. If you divide the 80,000,000-year age of Meiji volcano by 270 plant colonizations, the result is an astounding one successful arrival every 296,000 years! If you calculate using Kaua'i, the oldest of the eight main islands at 5,000,000 years, the result is one colonization per 18,500 years.

It was extremely difficult for viable seeds to reach the most isolated large group of islands on Earth. Another reason why successful colonizations were so rare was because the newly arrived propagules were exposed to harsh conditions, including scorching heat, drought, burning lava, hungry birds and lack of suitable soil or sand. If, by some rare chance, they found the right amounts of sunlight, nutrients, rainfall and pollinators, they might survive in this new environment.

Hawai'i has the most unique flora on Earth for its size. Eighty-nine percent of our native plant species are found nowhere else on the planet! These living masterpieces are the products of countless centuries of evolution and one of the finest treasures of Hawai'i's great biological heritage. They deserve our care and protection.

NATIVE
HAWAIIAN
COASTAL PLANT
SPECIES

The following is the list of native Hawaiian coastal plant species included in this guide (this list does not include all Hawaiian coastal plant species):

Acacia koa

Achyranthes splendens

Argemone glauca

Artemisia australis

Bacopa monnieri

Boerhavia repens

Brighamia insignis

Canavalia pubescens

Capparis sandwichiana

Centaurium sebaeoides

Chamaesyce celastroides

Chamaesyce degeneri

Chamaesyce skottsbergii

Chenopodium oahuense

Colubrina asiatica

Cressa truxillensis

Cuscuta sandwichiana

Cyperus trachysanthos

Diospyros sandwicensis

Dodonaea viscosa

Doryopteris decipiens

Eragrostis variabilis

Erythrina sandwicensis

Fimbristylis cymosa

Gossypium tomentosum

Hedyotis littoralis

Heliotropium anomalum

Heliotropium curassavicum

Heteropogon contortus

Ipomoea pes-caprae

Jacquemontia ovalifolia

Lepidium bidentatum

Lipochaeta integrifolia

Lipochaeta lobata

Lycium sandwicense

Lysimachia mauritiana

Marsilea villosa

Metrosideros polymorpha

Myoporum sandwicense

Nama sandwicensis

Nototrichium sandwicense

Osteomeles anthyllidifolia

Pandanus tectorius

Plectranthus parviflorus

Plumbago zeylanica

Portulaca lutea

Portulaca molokiniensis

Portulaca villosa

Pseudognaphalium sandwicensium

Psydrax odorata

Reynoldsia sandwicensis

Santalum ellipticum

Scaevola coriacea

Scaevola taccada

Schiedea adamantis

Schiedea globosa

Senna gaudichaudii

Sesbania tomentosa

Sesuvium portulacastrum

Sida fallax

Solanum nelsonii

Sporobolus virginicus

Tetramolopium rockii

Tribulus cistoides

Vigna marina

Vitex rotundifolia

Waltheria indica

Wikstroemia uva-ursi

Acacia koa
HAWAIIAN NAME: **Koa**
Endemic

IDENTIFICATION:

A large tree with wide spreading branches that grows to 115-feet tall. Some trees have trunk diameters exceeding 10-feet. The bark is furrowed and light gray. What appear to be leaves are really crescent shaped phyllodes or flattened leaf stems. The true leaflets are much smaller. Flowers are pale yellow.

DISTRIBUTION:

A dominant element of both the dry and wet forest that grows from 200 to 6,750-feet elevation on all the main islands except Niʻihau and Kahoʻolawe.

USES:

Koa was used for making Hawaiian canoes, spears, paddles, bowls and surf-boards.

ADDITIONAL INFORMATION:

Koa, meaning warrior in Hawaiian, is in the pea family. Known as the "Hawaiian mahogany" the wood is used today for making furniture, picture frames, musical instruments and jewelry boxes. The finest curly grain koa can sell for $45 a board foot. Considered to be the most important native Hawaiian forest tree.

Achyranthes splendens

HAWAIIAN NAME: None recorded.
Endemic

IDENTIFICATION:
Achyranthes splendens is a shrub that grows in height from 1½–6½-feet tall. Small flowers are contained in the terminal spikes. The silvery gray-ish-green leaves are covered by very fine hairs that help to counteract the intense sun and dry conditions where this species lives.

DISTRIBUTION:
Grows from sea level to 1,600-feet elevation in coastal areas on coralline plains and rocky slopes. Approximately 2,000–3,000 individuals in 4 populations existed on Oʻahu in 2001 according to the U.S. Fish and Wildlife Service. This species can also be found in low numbers on Maui, Molokaʻi and Lanaʻi.

USES:
None reported.

ADDITIONAL INFORMATION:
Also called the round-leaf chaff flower. This species is in the amaranth family.

Argemone glauca
HAWAIIAN NAME: Pua kala
Endemic

IDENTIFICATION:
Plants are 1–4-feet high. Flowers have 6 large white petals and an orange center with a red pistil, which is the female organ of the flower. Leaves, stems and buds are covered by sharp spines and have a grayish appearance.

DISTRIBUTION:
Found in dry rocky areas from 0 to 6,000-feet on leeward sides of all main islands.

USES:
Hawaiians used the sap of the stem to treat toothaches, backaches, nerve-related diseases and ulcers. It was also used as an ingredient to treat tuberculosis.

ADDITIONAL INFORMATION:
The Hawaiian poppy is unusual because it is biennial, meaning it completes its entire life cycle in two years. Most native Hawaiian plant species are perennial, which means they live more than two years. The pua kala is closely related to North and South American poppy species and is believed to have arrived in the Hawaiian Islands only several thousand years ago. The seeds can resist fire. This species was observed by Captain Cook in 1779.

Artemisia australis
HAWAIIAN NAME: 'Āhinahina,
Hinahina kuahiwi
Endemic

IDENTIFICATION:
A fine-leaved shrub 2–5-feet high.

DISTRIBUTION:
Occurs on cliff faces from sea level to 3,500-feet elevation mainly on the windward sides of all the main islands.

USES:
Leaves, stalks and roots, mixed with other ingredients, were made into a steam bath used to treat fever. Leaves alone, in conjunction with other ingredients, were taken orally as a treatment for asthma.

ADDITIONAL INFORMATION:
The small shrubs have a faint aroma. This species is derived from a North American sagebrush that colonized Hawai'i in pre-human times.

Bacopa monnieri
HAWAIIAN NAME: **ʻAeʻae**
Indigenous

IDENTIFICATION:
An aquatic or semi-aquatic perennial herb that forms mats. Leaves are succulent, spatula-shaped and 0.2–0.8-inches long. The flowers are pale blue, pinkish or white.

DISTRIBUTION:
Occurs on sand, rocks, mud flats and in marshes or brackish streams on all the main islands, except Kahoʻolawe, from sea level to 750-feet elevation.

USES:
No traditional Hawaiian uses reported.

ADDITIONAL INFORMATION:
Also called the water hyssop. This species is now used frequently as a ground cover. According to herbal medicine experts, *Bacopa* assists in heightening mental acuity and is considered the main rejuvenating herb for nerve and brain cells.

Boerhavia repens
HAWAIIAN NAME: **Alena**
Indigenous

IDENTIFICATION:
Perennial herbs with pink stems that grow along the ground. Leaves are $1/2$–$1^1/_2$-inches long. Flowers are tiny, pinkish and tubular.

DISTRIBUTION:
Grows on lava flows, beaches and rocky slopes in moderately dry coastal areas.

USES:
Hawaiians used this plant medicinally. In Australia, Fiji and Samoa the root is eaten by natives.

ADDITIONAL INFORMATION:
This species most likely arrived in Hawai'i when the sticky seeds became attached to migratory shorebirds.

ENDANGERED

Brighamia insignis
HAWAIIAN NAME: **ʻŌlulu**
Endemic

IDENTIFICATION:

Thick, succulent stem 3–6-feet tall that is bulbous at the bottom and tapers toward the top. The fleshy leaves measure 5–7-inches long and 2–4-inches wide. Fragrant yellow flowers grow in groups of 3–8.

DISTRIBUTION:

Found on sea cliffs from sea level to 1,400-feet elevation on Niʻihau and Kauaʻi.

USES:

None reported.

ADDITIONAL INFORMATION:

The ʻōlulu was designated as endangered on February 25, 1994. The plant is described as a cabbage on a stick. As few as 20 plants of this species remain in the wild.

Canavalia pubescens

'Āwikiwiki

Endemic

IDENTIFICATION:
A perennial climbing vine with stunning dark red flowers that have white streaks near the base and large green seed pods. A dense covering of velvety hairs gives the plant a silvery appearance.

DISTRIBUTION:
Found in dry forest or on open lava fields from 50–1,750-feet elevation.

USES:
None reported.

ADDITIONAL INFORMATION:
Canavalia pubescens is listed as a candidate for endangered species listing. Only 10 populations exist on Maui, Lāna'i, Kaua'i and possibly Ni'ihau, with approximately 200 individual plants remaining.

Capparis sandwichiana
HAWAIIAN NAME: Maiapilo
Endemic

IDENTIFICATION:
A small shrub that grows 2–3-feet high with beautiful, fragrant white-petaled flowers, which open at night and fade just after sunrise.

DISTRIBUTION:
Very uncommon on lava flows and sandy areas from sea level to 350-feet elevation.

USES:
Hawaiians used this species as a cure for broken bones.

ADDITIONAL INFORMATION:
Capparis sandwichiana is a close relative of *Capparis spinosa* that grows in the Mediterranean region and from which the pungent flower buds are pickled and eaten as capers.

Centaurium sebaeoides

ENDANGERED

HAWAIIAN NAME: 'Āwiwi

Endemic

IDENTIFICATION:
This delicate annual herb grows from 2–8-inches high and has very small white flowers.

DISTRIBUTION:
Scattered and very rare in dry coastal areas where it grows on rocky, volcanic or clay soil.

USES:
None reported.

ADDITIONAL INFORMATION:
On October 29, 1991, the 'āwiwi was designated as endangered.

ENDANGERED

Chamaesyce celastroides varkaenana
HAWAIIAN NAME: **'Akoko**
Endemic

IDENTIFICATION:
This shrub is a member of the spurge family and is a shortlived perennial that grows up to 5-feet high. It has a milky sap and leaves, arranged in two opposite rows along the stem, that fall off during the summer.

DISTRIBUTION:
Grows from sea level to 2,800-feet on both rocky and grassy slopes.

USES:
None reported.

ADDITIONAL INFORMATION:
Less than 600 plants of this species remain in the wild.

Chamaesyce degeneri
HAWAIIAN NAME: **ʻAkoko or Koko**
Endemic

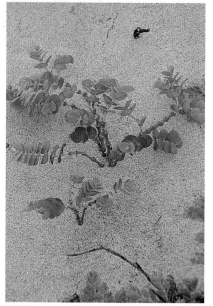

IDENTIFICATION:
This species grows along the ground as a sprawling mat. It has succulent, rounded, inch-long leaves that turn red. Flowers are yellow and very small.

DISTRIBUTION:
A uncommon component of beach and coastal vegetation from 0–175-feet on all main islands except Lānaʻi and Kahoʻolawe.

USES:
The Hawaiians apparently did not have any uses for this plant.

ADDITIONAL INFORMATION:
The name ʻakoko means "blood-colored" in Hawaiian and refers to this species' red leaves. The small seeds of this species float easily in seawater. Named in honor of Otto Degener (1899–1988), a noted botanist who taught at the University of Hawaiʻi and wrote *Flora Hawaiiensis*, one of the most important books about Hawaiian plants.

Chamaesyce skottsbergii
HAWAIIAN NAME: **'Akoko**
Endemic

IDENTIFICATION:
Slender branches with small round- or oblong-shaped blue-green leaves that turn red. Mostly low lying and mat-forming but this species can grow 6-feet high. Tiny yellow flowers grow at the base of each leaf.

DISTRIBUTION:
Grows on sandstone and lava ledges and in shallow sand on Moloka'i and O'ahu.

USES:
None reported.

ADDITIONAL INFORMATION:
This rare species was named after Carl Skottsberg (1880–1963), a Swedish professor of botany who collected the type specimen in 1922 from the 'Ewa coral plain on O'ahu.

Chenopodium oahuense
HAWAIIAN NAME: **'Āheahea**
Endemic

IDENTIFICATION:
Shrubs that can grow to 6-feet. The thick leaves are $^3/_4$ –$1^1/_2$-inches wide and $^1/_2$–1-inch long.

DISTRIBUTION:
Somewhat common in dry coastal habitats and sub-alpine shrubland from sea level up to 8,000-feet.

USES:
The leaves of young plants were cooked and eaten during times of food scarcity. The wood was used to make fishhooks.

ADDITIONAL INFORMATION:
'Āheahea is a member of the goosefoot family.

Colubrina asiatica
HAWAIIAN NAME: **ʻĀnapanapa**
Indigenous

IDENTIFICATION:
A shrub with twining stems that can grow 20-feet high and has 2–3-inch long heart-shaped leaves. The yellow-green flowers are very small and found in clusters.

DISTRIBUTION:
Occurs in coastal areas from sea level to 325-feet elevation.

USES:
This species' common name is "latherleaf" because its leaves form a lather in water and were used as soap. In Asia, it is also used for food, medicine and fish poison.

ADDITIONAL INFORMATION:
This member of the buckthorn family is widely distributed from India, Africa, Australia and Polynesia. The salt-tolerant seeds can float long distances in ocean currents. The Hawaiian name ʻānapanapa means "glistening." The latin name *colubrina* means "snake-like."

Cressa truxillensis

HAWAIIAN NAME: **None recorded.**
Indigenous

IDENTIFICATION:
A small herb that grows 2–14-inches high. The white flowers are very small.

DISTRIBUTION:
Found in alkaline soils, drying mudflats and sand along and behind beaches on Kahoʻolawe, Molokaʻi and possibly on Oʻahu.

USES:
None reported.

ADDITIONAL INFORMATION:
A member of the Morning glory family *Convolvulaceae*. The scientific name *Cressa* refers to a Cretan woman named Kressa. *Truxillensis* apparently is a reference to the city of Trujillo in Peru, where *C. truxillensis* was first described.

Cuscuta sandwichiana
HAWAIIAN NAME: Kauna'oa
Endemic

IDENTIFICATION:
Has threadlike yellowish-orange stems without leaves. The flowers are very small, compact and have five whitish-yellow petals. The fruits contain small reddish seeds. Immature plants have roots but these disintegrate quickly and the mature plants are not attached to the ground.

DISTRIBUTION:
Found on all the main islands except Kaua'i and Kaho'olawe from sea level to 900-feet elevation.

USES:
Kauna'oa is used to make orange leis. It was also given to women after childbirth and to treat chest colds.

ADDITIONAL INFORMATION:
Called the Hawaiian dodder, this is the official flower of Lāna'i. The scientific name, *Cuscuta*, means "tangled twist of hair," in Arabic. In the old literature it was called "the motherless plant" because it is a parasite that attaches itself to other plants to obtain its nutrients.

Cyperus trachysanthos

ENDANGERED

HAWAIIAN NAME: Pu'uka'a

Endemic

IDENTIFICATION:
A member of the sedge family (*Cyperaceae*), this species is a perennial grass-like plant with a short rhizome (underground stem). It grows 8–18-inches tall.

DISTRIBUTION:
Occurs in wet areas, on coastal cliffs or talus slopes from 10–525-feet elevation. Currently this species is known from 3 populations on Ni'ihau, Kaua'i and O'ahu with an estimated total of less than 350 individuals.

USES:
Pu'uka'a was used to make baskets and sleeping mats.

ADDITIONAL INFORMATION:
Also called umbrella sedge. *Trachysanthos* refers to the rough or papery flowers. With permission, this species can be seen at Diamond Head Crater State Park. On October 10, 1996, the pu'uka'a was declared an endangered species by the United States Fish and Wildlife Service.

Diospyros sandwicensis
HAWAIIAN NAME: Lama

Endemic

IDENTIFICATION:
Trees 6–32-feet tall with pale green 1–5-inch long leaves and black bark. The fruit, somewhat like a persimmon, is yellow to reddish-orange.

DISTRIBUTION:
Found on all the main islands except Niʻihau and Kahoʻolawe from 15–4,000-feet elevation.

USES:
The persimmon-like fruit was eaten. The highly-prized hard reddish-brown wood of this species was used by Hawaiians to build temples and fish traps and fence sacred areas. Pulverized lama was used as an ingredient for treating skin ulcers. A block of lama wood, wrapped in yellow tapa cloth, represented the hula goddess Laka.

ADDITIONAL INFORMATION:
This species is in the ebony family. Lama means "light" or "enlightenment."

Dodonaea viscosa
HAWAIIAN NAME: **'A'ali'i**
Indigenous

IDENTIFICATION:
These shrubs or trees can grow from 1–20-feet high. Leaves have a sticky covering. The best way to identify this species is the bright red or yellow fruit clusters.

DISTRIBUTION:
Grows in open areas on coastal dunes, lava flows and mountain ridges from 10–7,500-feet elevation.

USES:
Fruits and leaves were used in lei making. The hard, yellow-brown wood is very durable and was used to make digging sticks, spears and building materials. The red capsules were used to make red dye. Tips from 'a'ali'i branches were used to treat asthma.

ADDITIONAL INFORMATION:
Also called the Hawaiian hop bush. The 'a'ali'i was sacred to the hula goddess Laka.

Doryopteris decipiens
HAWAIIAN NAME: ʻIwaʻiwa
Endemic

IDENTIFICATION:
This native fern can grow up to 15-inches tall. The fronds are medium to dull green.

DISTRIBUTION:
Grows in clusters in dry, exposed rocky areas from 400–3,000-feet.

USES:
None reported.

ADDITIONAL INFORMATION:
The species name means "deceptive."

Eragrostis variabilis
HAWAIIAN NAMES: **Kāwelu, 'Emoloa and Kalamālō**
Endemic

IDENTIFICATION:
A perennial grass that grows from 16–32-inches tall.

DISTRIBUTION:
Occurs on sand dunes and exposed cliffs from sea level to 3,700-feet.

USES:
Kāwelu was one of several native grasses used for thatching in the construction of Hawaiian homes.

ADDITIONAL INFORMATION:
Also called lovegrass. It is often referred to in Hawaiian hula chants and local poetry. Native birds eat the seeds and use this grass for nesting material.

Erythrina sandwicensis
HAWAIIAN NAMES: **Wiliwili**

Endemic

IDENTIFICATION:

This beautiful native tree has a short, gnarled trunk, grows from 15–55-feet tall and drops its leaves in summer. It was once an important component of ancient endemic Hawaiian dryland forests (Rock 1913). The orange, furrowed bark has $^1/_2$-inch long thorns. The flowers, representing a striking color variation in this species, are red, orange, yellow, white or pale green. Seeds are a bright red.

DISTRIBUTION:

Grows from near sea level to 2,000-feet elevation on the dry, leeward sides of all the major islands.

USES:

The soft, balsa-like wood was used to make fishing floats and canoe outriggers. Early Hawaiian surfboards, measuring 20-feet long and weighing 175 pounds, were made from these trees. The seeds are used to make leis.

ADDITIONAL INFORMATION:

The Hawaiian name means "twisted-twisted." Also called the Hawaiian coral tree. *Erythrina sandwicensis* is closely related to both the *E. tahitensis* and *E. velutina*. A spectacular tree measured on the island of Hawai'i in 1968 was 55-feet tall with a trunk circumference of 12.$^1/_2$-feet.

Fimbristylis cymosa
HAWAIIAN NAME: Mau'u

Indigenous

IDENTIFICATION:
A tufted, perennial sedge that can grow 12-inches high. The culms or aerial stems are very stiff. Small flowers are found on the long stalks above the leaves.

DISTRIBUTION:
Common on sandy beaches and lava flows across the Pacific region from sea level to 200-feet elevation.

USES:
The stems were reportedly used to clean the ears.

ADDITIONAL INFORMATION:
The endangered Laysan finch, which only occurs on remote Laysan Island, eats the seeds of mau'u.

Gossypium tomentosum
HAWAIIAN NAME: Ma'o, Huluhulu
Endemic

IDENTIFICATION:

A low shrub 2–5-feet in height. Leaves are $1^{1}/_{2}$–2-inches long and three lobed. Flowers have five yellow petals. Seeds are covered by a reddish-brown lint.

DISTRIBUTION:

Occurs in arid, rocky coastal areas on all the main islands except Hawai'i from sea level to 400-feet elevation.

USES:

Leaves were used to make green dye and the flower petals for yellow dye.

ADDITIONAL INFORMATION:

This is a native Hawaiian cotton plant. The short brownish fibers on the seeds of the Hawaiian cotton are not commercially useful but the Hawaiian plants' genes have been used in cotton breeding programs in attempts to improve disease resistance and drought tolerance in commercial cotton.

The genus *Gossypium* consists of 39 species, 4 of which are cultivated. The most commonly cultivated species is *G. hirsutum*. Other cultivated species are *G. arboreum*, *G. barbadense* and *G. herbaceum*. Four species of *Gossypium* occur in the United States. *Gossypium hirsutum* is the primary cultivated cotton. *Gossypium barbadense* is also cultivated. The other two species, *G. thurberi* and *G. tomentosum* are wild plants of Arizona and Hawai'i.

Hedyotis littoralis
HAWAIIAN NAME: None recorded.
Endemic

IDENTIFICATION:
Succulent perennial herbs with small, white star-shaped flowers usually having four petals.

DISTRIBUTION:
Occurs on wet, rocky sea cliffs from 6–20-feet elevation on Maui, Moloka'i and Hawai'i. Formerly on O'ahu.

USES:
None reported.

ADDITIONAL INFORMATION:
This rare species is a member of the coffee family. The Latin name *Hedyotis* is derived from the Latin words *hedys* meaning sweet and *otus*, ear, in reference to the sweet smelling leaves of some species of *Hedyotis*.

Heliotropium anomalum
HAWAIIAN NAME: **Hinahina**
Indigenous

IDENTIFICATION:
This perennial grows close to the ground. The $^1/_2$–1-inch green/gray leaves are covered by fine silky hairs which gives the hinahina a silver appearance. Tiny white fragrant flowers with yellow centers are found in clusters.

DISTRIBUTION:
Found in dry coastal areas growing on sandy beaches and bluffs.

USES:
The flowers are used in lei making. This species was also used to make medicinal tea.

ADDITIONAL INFORMATION:
Heliotropium is derived from the Greek words *helios* meaning "sun" and *trope* meaning "turning," which refers to the incorrect belief that the flowers turn to face the sun.

Heliotropium curassavicum
HAWAIIAN NAME: **Kīpūkai**
Indigenous

IDENTIFICATION:
A perennial herb with thick, narrow 1-inch leaves that grow between 1–2-feet long. Very small white flowers grow in clusters and have a green or yellow center.

DISTRIBUTION:
Occurs in alkaline flats and along sea coast.

USES:
Leaves were used for a medicinal tea.

ADDITIONAL INFORMATION:
Also called the seaside heliotrope.

Heteropogon contortus
HAWAIIAN NAME: Pili

Indigenous or perhaps a Polynesian introduction.

IDENTIFICATION:
A perennial grass that forms tufts as high as 3 feet and grows in large bunches. The blades are a pale bluish-green.

DISTRIBUTION:
Occurs on dry rocky cliffs and ledges from sea level to 2,000-feet.

USES:
The blades from the pili grass were burnt and the charcoal was used to make black dye. This species was formerly used as the preferred thatch to cover Hawaiian homes because of its pleasant odor and neat appearance. The pili covering had to be replaced after 4–5 years.

ADDITIONAL INFORMATION:
Also called "twisted beardgrass" or "tangle-head grass." Pili is quickly disappearing from much of its former range on both Oʻahu and Molokaʻi.

Ipomoea pes-caprae
HAWAIIAN NAME: Pōhuehue

Indigenous

IDENTIFICATION:
A trailing vine that grows up to 16-feet long. Leaves are thick and broad and between 2–4-inches long. The impressive bell-shaped flowers are pink or light purple with a darker purple center.

DISTRIBUTION:
Occurs on beaches and occasionally inland from sea level to 1,500-feet elevation.

USES:
Small amounts of the roots and leaves were used as a famine food. Used as an ingredient in preparations to treat lung trouble, sprains and as a blood cleanser.

ADDITIONAL INFORMATION:
Pōhuehue is a member of the morning glory family. Most of its flowers open in the morning. Its seeds float easily in salt water.

Jacquemontia ovalifolia
HAWAIIAN NAME: **Pā'ūohi'iaka**
Endemic

IDENTIFICATION:
A flat-lying perennial vine that grows up to 10-feet in length with 1–1¹/₂-inch long leaves. The cup-shaped flowers are pale-blue to white.

DISTRIBUTION:
Mostly found on the leeward side of the main islands from sea level to 100-feet elevation.

USES:
Hawaiians used the stems and leaves as a cathartic and for treating babies with thrush.

ADDITIONAL INFORMATION:
A member of the morning glory family. The Hawaiian name, which means "skirt of Hi'iaka," is derived from a legend that tells how Hi'iaka, the younger sister of Pele, was sleeping on the beach and this plant covered her to protect her from sunburn.

Lepidium bidentatum
HAWAIIAN NAME: **'Ānaunau**
Indigenous

IDENTIFICATION:

This shrub can grow up to 24-inches high. The $1\frac{1}{2}$–3-inch long leaves are thick and fleshy. The small flowers have 4 white petals.

DISTRIBUTION:

This species is found on all the main islands except Ni'ihau and Kaho'olawe from 0–800-feet elevation in coastal locations and on dry, steep cliffs.

USES:

In the Society Islands, the leaves are eaten.

ADDITIONAL INFORMATION:

European explorers sailing in the Pacific ate this plant to prevent scurvy. A rare endemic variety, *o-waihiense*, occurs only on several of the remote northwestern Hawaiian Islands. When the seeds of *Lepidium bidentatum* get wet, they form a sticky coating that helps them get attached to bird feathers.

Lipochaeta integrifolia

HAWAIIAN NAME: Nehe

Endemic

IDENTIFICATION:
A low-lying perennial that can grow 6–12-inches above the ground. The inch long, whitish-green leaves are somewhat fleshy. The small flowers average ¹/₂ inch in diameter.

DISTRIBUTION:
Grows on sand or lava outcrops along the coast of Kure Atoll, Laysan and all the main Hawaiian Islands.

USES:
None reported.

ADDITIONAL INFORMATION:
The genus *Lipochaeta* had 20 species endemic to the Hawaiian Islands, many of which are endangered or extinct.

Lipochaeta lobata var. lobata
HAWAIIAN NAME: Nehe

Endemic

IDENTIFICATION:
A perennial that grows from 20–60-inches high. Leaves are 1½–3-inches long. Flowers have yellow petals.

DISTRIBUTION:
Occurs in dry coastal areas from sea level to 1,200-feet.

USES:
None reported.

ADDITIONAL INFORMATION:
This species is in the sunflower family.

Lycium sandwicense
HAWAIIAN NAME: **ʻŌhelo kai**
Indigenous

IDENTIFICATION:
A low spreading shrub that grows from a few inches above the ground up to 3-feet tall. The green, 1-inch long, succulent leaves are alternately located on the stem. Flowers are pale lavender, tubular in shape and have 4 petals. The most conspicuous feature of this plant is the bright red berries.

DISTRIBUTION:
Occurs from sea level to 130-feet elevation growing in salt marshes and in rocky coastal locations.

USES:
The salty berries are occasionally eaten.

ADDITIONAL INFORMATION:
In Hawaiian, ʻōhelo kai means "sea berry." This species is endemic to Polynesia and belongs to the genus *Solanaceae* that also includes the tomato and potato.

Lysimachia mauritiana

HAWAIIAN NAME: None recorded.

Indigenous

IDENTIFICATION:

A very rare, somewhat succulent perennial herb with light
green fleshy leaves and white
flower clusters. Stems are
4–30-inches long.

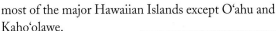

DISTRIBUTION:

Grows on sea cliffs, gravel
beaches and coastal rocks
from 6–30-feet elevation on
most of the major Hawaiian Islands except Oʻahu and
Kahoʻolawe.

USES:

None reported.

**ADDITIONAL
INFORMATION:**

Lysimachia is in the
primrose family.

Marsilea villosa

ENDANGERED

HAWAIIAN NAME: **ʻIhiʻihi**

Endemic

IDENTIFICATION:
Looks like a 4-leaf clover. The plant occurs either in scattered clumps or as a dense mat.

DISTRIBUTION:
Located in flat lowland areas where seasonal flooding occurs.

USES:
None reported.

ADDITIONAL INFORMATION:
This fern was federally listed as endangered on June 22, 1992. There are four known populations of this species with fewer than 2,000 individual plants.

Metrosideros polymorpha
HAWAIIAN NAME: ʻŌhiʻa
Endemic

IDENTIFICATION:

Small shrubs or trees that grow to 100-feet tall with umbrella-like crowns and bright red flowers that have numerous stamens. Flowers can also be salmon, pink, yellow or rarely white. Young leaves are reddish and older leaves are dull or shiny green.

DISTRIBUTION:

Occurs from near sea level to 7,200-feet as a tree or small shrub on all the main islands except Niʻihau and Kahoʻolawe.

USES:

The sacred ʻōhiʻa was the primary wood used for carving temple god images. It was also used to make musical instruments, canoe seats and gunwales. The flowers and young leaves were strung on leis.

ADDITIONAL INFORMATION:

This is the most abundant and widespread native tree in Hawaiʻi. Today, the dark red wood is used for flooring, fenceposts and fuel. The seeds of ʻōhiʻa are very small and might have originally arrived in the Hawaiian Islands via air flotation. In battle, the first Hawaiian killed was called "lehua," a possible reference to the spilled blood of the fallen warrior being similar to the red flower of this tree.

Myoporum sandwicense
HAWAIIAN NAME: **Naio**
Endemic

IDENTIFICATION:
Small to large trees from 3–35-feet tall with dark gray, grooved bark. The pointed, succulent leaves are 2–6-inches long. The small pinkish-white flowers have 5 petals. Naio wood is dark yellow-green, very hard and scented like sandalwood.

DISTRIBUTION:
From sea level to 7,800-feet elevation.

USES:
The durable wood was used for gauges for making fish nets and for posts in house construction. The leaf buds were one ingredient used in a medicine to treat asthma. Dry powdered naio was used to treat growths in the nose and for lung trouble.

ADDITIONAL INFORMATION:
This species is called "bastard sandalwood" because it was substituted for the more valuable sandalwood when supplies were exhausted.

Nama sandwicensis
HAWAIIAN NAME: Hinahina kahakai

Endemic

IDENTIFICATION:
Forms mats 2–10-inches in diameter and $^1/_2$–1-inch high. Purplish-blue flowers have white or yellow throats. The deep green, succulent leaves are slightly cupped and 1$^1/_2$-inches long.

DISTRIBUTION:
Uncommon on raised limestone reefs and sandy soils from sea level to 700-feet elevation.

USES:
None reported.

ADDITIONAL INFORMATION:
Nama is the Greek word for "spring."

Nototrichium sandwicense
HAWAIIAN NAME: **Kuluʻī**
Endemic

IDENTIFICATION:
A large shrub or small tree that can grow up to 15-feet tall with silver-gray leaves and drooping spikes with minute flowers. All parts are covered by silky, silvery hairs.

DISTRIBUTION:
Found on lava fields and exposed ridges in dry areas from sea level to 2,400-feet elevation on all of the main islands.

USES:
None reported.

ADDITIONAL INFORMATION:
This species is in the amaranth family.

Osteomeles anthyllidifolia
HAWAIIAN NAME: ʻŪlei
Indigenous

IDENTIFICATION:
Shrubs up to 10-feet tall with ³/₄ –2³/₄-inch long leaves and white flowers with five petals. The berries are whitish-purple.

DISTRIBUTION:
Found on coastal cliffs, lava fields and in dry shrub land from 6–7,500-feet elevation on all the main islands except Kahoʻolawe and Niʻihau.

USES:
The hard wood was made into a digging stick called the ʻōʻō and fish spears. Branches were used for baskets and fish nets. The sweet tasting berries were eaten, used to make lavender dye and made into leis.

ADDITIONAL INFORMATION:
ʻŪlei is a member of the rose family.

Pandanus tectorius
HAWAIIAN NAME: **Hala**
Indigenous

IDENTIFICATION:
A shrub or tree that can grow up to 30-feet tall with aerial prop roots. Twisted, thorny, sharp-pointed leaves called *lau hala* are 30–70-inches long and up to 2-inches wide. The large fruit, which consists of 50 or more wedge-shaped yellow drupes, looks like a pineapple. The long yellow flowers are fragrant.

DISTRIBUTION:
Found from sea level to 2,000-feet altitude.

USES:
The tips of the roots were used as medicine. Leaves were plaited to make floor and sleeping mats, fans, sandals, baskets and pillows. The drupes, or "keys," were used as paintbrushes and in leimaking.

ADDITIONAL INFORMATION:
Also called the "screwpine" and the "walking tree" because of the aerial roots.

Plectranthus parviflorus
HAWAIIAN NAME: **ʻAlaʻala wai nui**
Indigenous

IDENTIFICATION:
Perennial shrubs with somewhat fleshy stems and branches. The small flowers are white and pale blue.

DISTRIBUTION:
Occurs from sea level to 4,200-feet elevation in rocky locations on all the main islands except Kahoʻolawe.

USES:
None reported.

ADDITIONAL INFORMATION:
In the mint family, but the foliage is not aromatic. Also called the "spurflower."

Plumbago zeylanica
HAWAIIAN NAME: **'Ilie'e**
Indigenous

IDENTIFICATION:
A sprawling shrub up to 6-feet long. Can be mistaken for a vine. Flowers are white and slightly less than $1/2$-inch long.

DISTRIBUTION:
Occurs from sea level to 2,000-feet elevation growing in sand dunes, arid shrub lands and dry forest areas.

USES:
Juice from the roots was used as tattoo pigment.

ADDITIONAL INFORMATION:
The name *Plumbago* is derived from the Greek words *plumbum* meaning "lead" and *agere* meaning "to convey." A possible reference to the blue-gray color left on the hands when touching the roots. This plant is poisonous if eaten.

Portulaca lutea
HAWAIIAN NAME: 'Ihi
Indigenous

IDENTIFICATION:
Perennial herbs 3–12 inches tall with large, 5-petaled, yellow flowers and rounded succulent leaves $^1/_2$–1- inch long arranged alternately on the stems.

DISTRIBUTION:
Grows on sandy beaches and raised limestone or lava rock from sea level to 130-feet elevation.

USES:
None reported.

ADDITIONAL INFORMATION:
The stems and leaves of this species float in seawater helping it to colonize many of the Hawaiian Islands.

Portulaca molokiniensis
HAWAIIAN NAME: **'Ihi**
Endemic

IDENTIFICATION:
An upright plant growing to 12-inches tall with very succulent leaves. The flowers are lemon-yellow and occur at the tips of the stems.

DISTRIBUTION:
In coastal sites growing in volcanic tuff and on steep rocky slopes from 30–375-feet elevation. This rare species only grows on two small islets off Maui and one location on Kaho'olawe.

USES:
None reported.

ADDITIONAL INFORMATION:
Portulaca molokiniensis is closely related to *P. Iutea* and probably derived from it.

Portulaca villosa
HAWAIIAN NAME: 'Ihi
Endemic

IDENTIFICATION:
Succulent perennial herbs with stems up to 12-inches long. Leaves are pale grayish-green. Flowers are white with pink margins and approximately an inch in diameter.

DISTRIBUTION:
Occurs on dry lava, clay or raised limestone reef sites from sea level to 1,000-feet elevation.

USES:
None reported.

ADDITIONAL INFORMATION:
This rare species is one of three endemic *Portulaca* found only in the Hawaiian Islands.

Pseudognaphalium sandwicensium
HAWAIIAN NAME: **'Ena'ena**
Endemic

IDENTIFICATION:

A small plant that grows to 24-inches tall and is covered with soft white hairs. Flowers are a dark yellow.

DISTRIBUTION:

In dry locations growing on clay or dunes from sea level to almost 10,000-feet elevation.

USES:

As an insect repellent when storing feather work.

ADDITIONAL INFORMATION:

Four varieties of this species exist in Hawai'i. 'Ena'ena is a member of the sunflower family and its common name is cudweed.

Psydrax odorata
HAWAIIAN NAME: Alaheʻe
Indigenous

IDENTIFICATION:
A medium to large shrub that can attain small tree proportions. Grows from 2–20-feet tall. The small, $1/4$-inch long, white flowers are fragrant and the fruits are black. The leaves are 2–3-inches long and shiny.

DISTRIBUTION:
This species occurs in dry shrubland and in mountain forests from 30–2,800-feet elevation.

USES:
The hard wood of alaheʻe was used for a digging stick called ʻōʻō, spears, fishhooks and for adze blades. A black dye was made from the leaves.

ADDITIONAL INFORMATION:
The latin name *odorata* refers to the perfumed flowers.

Reynoldsia sandwicensis
HAWAIIAN NAME: 'Ohe makai
Endemic

IDENTIFICATION:
Trees up to 65-feet tall with a spreading crown, straight trunk and dark purple fruit. The thick branches appear to be succulent. Leaves fall off in summer.

DISTRIBUTION:
Occurs in dry forest from 100–2,600-feet elevation.

USES:
The yellowish resin was used by the early Hawaiians.

ADDITIONAL INFORMATION:
Named after J.N.Reynolds, an early 19th century plant collector. This species is declining over most of its range. As recently as 1940, a few of these majestic trees could be found in the vicinity of Koko Crater, O'ahu.

Santalum ellipticum
HAWAIIAN NAME: **'Iliahialo'e**
Endemic

IDENTIFICATION:
Shrubs to small trees growing from 3–15-feet high with succulent dull greenish-gray leaves and a rounded shape. Flowers have a sweet fragrance. The greenish petals are tinged with brown, salmon or orange. The fruits are purple-black.

DISTRIBUTION:
Grows on dry coastal ridges or in gulches from sea level to 1,800-feet elevation.

USES:
An ingredient in a Hawaiian herbal medication used to treat joint aches. The powdered heartwood was used to scent tapa cloth.

ADDITIONAL INFORMATION:
Sandalwood trees are parasitic and they partly depend on other plants for nutrients. The genus *Santalum* includes 25 species.

ENDANGERED

Scaevola coriacea

HAWAIIAN NAME: Naupaka papa

Endemic

IDENTIFICATION:
Low, flat-lying perennial herb. The succulent leaves are oval, or spatula-shaped with smooth, rounded tips. The small flowers have white petals.

DISTRIBUTION:
Occurs in dry coastal sites on low, consolidated sand dunes near sea level.

USES:
None reported.

ADDITIONAL INFORMATION:
This species was historically found on 6 of the Hawaiian Islands but now only exists on Maui and 2 off-shore islets with less than 300 individuals. On May 16, 1986, the "dwarf naupaka" was designated as endangered.

Scaevola taccada

HAWAIIAN NAME: Naupaka kahakai

Indigenous

IDENTIFICATION:
Shrubs grow to 3–10-feet with bright green succulent leaves. The fragrant flowers are white, often with purple streaks, and appear to have been split in two with 5 petals remaining on one side.

DISTRIBUTION:
Occurs on coasts throughout the tropical Pacific and Indian Oceans.

USES:
The powdered bark was used to treat skin diseases and the leaves as a remedy for indigestion and beriberi. The berries are edible. The durable wood was used for pegs in shipbuilding.

ADDITIONAL INFORMATION:
According to one version of the many myths associated with the naupaka, the flower was once full but was torn in half by a princess who gave one half to her warrior husband who died in battle. Today the flower grows as a symbol of their love. Commonly used as a landscaping plant. Another Hawaiian name for this species is *huahekili*, meaning "hailstones," which is a reference to the white berries.

Schiedea adamantis

ENDANGERED

HAWAIIAN NAME: Māʻoliʻoli

Endemic

IDENTIFICATION:
A branching, brittle shrub 11–32-inches tall. Leaves are ¹/₂–1¹/₂-inches long.

DISTRIBUTION:
The last wild population remaining on Earth consisting of only 3 individuals grows on the southeast coast of Oʻahu approximately 400-feet above sea level. This population, once consisting of over 300 plants, has been decimated by a prolonged drought since 1988. *Schiedea adamantis* is highly endangered and the area where they grow is closed to the public.

USES:
None reported.

ADDITIONAL INFORMATION:
The Latin word *adamantis* means "diamond." *Schiedea adamantis* was listed as a Federal endangered species in February 1984. Current threats to the plant include drought, fire, competition from alien plants, disturbances by hikers, lack of native pollinators and an insect called thrips.

Schiedea globosa
HAWAIIAN NAME: None recorded.
Endemic

IDENTIFICATION:
Low sub shrubs that form clumps and grow between 2–8-inches tall. The thick leaves are opposite on the stems, fleshy and 1–3-inches long.

DISTRIBUTION:
Occurs on steep cliffs or rocky slopes from sea level to 1,000-feet elevation on Oʻahu, Molokaʻi and Maui.

USES:
None reported.

ADDITIONAL INFORMATION:
The Hawaiian plant genus *Schiedea* is endemic to the Hawaiian Islands and currently consists of 33 species, all of which are believed derived from a single ancestor. The genus was named in honor of Christian J. Schiedea, a German-born physician who collected in Mexico.

Senna gaudichaudii
HAWAIIAN NAME: **Kolomona**
Indigenous

IDENTIFICATION:
Shrubs growing from $1^{1}/_{2}$ –10-feet tall with 1–$2^{3}/_{4}$-inch long leaflets arranged in pairs. Flowers are greenish-white to pale yellow. The pods are brown and up to 6-inches long and $^{1}/_{2}$-inch wide.

DISTRIBUTION:
Occurs primarily in leeward locations on all the main islands except Ni'ihau and Kaho'olawe, growing on lava flows or talus slopes from 15–3,000-feet elevation.

USES:
None reported.

ADDITIONAL INFORMATION:
This species is in the pea family. *Senna* is the Latin form of an Arabic word that means "thorny bush."

Sesbania tomentosa
HAWAIIAN NAME: 'Ohai
Endemic

IDENTIFICATION:
A sprawling shrub with branches up to 45-feet long, but may also be a small tree up to 25-feet tall. Each leaf is made of many oval leaflets which appear silvery because they are densely covered with hairs. The flowers, growing in clusters of 2–9, are salmon, orange-red, scarlet or, rarely, pure yellow.

DISTRIBUTION:
Formerly occurred on all the main islands in low elevation dry areas, but today survives in only a few places growing on sand dunes, beaches and in soil pockets on lava flows from sea level to 2,700-feet elevation.

USES:
None reported.

ADDITIONAL INFORMATION:
On November 10, 1994, the 'ohai was listed as an endangered species. *Sesbania tomentosa* is a member of the pea family.

Sesuvium portulacastrum
HAWAIIAN NAME: ʻĀkulikuli
Indigenous

IDENTIFICATION:
A prostrate, succulent herb with trailing branches and fleshy red or green stems. Leaves are $^1/_4$ –$1^1/_2$-inch long, rounded and narrow. The small flowers are white to pale violet and have 5 petals.

DISTRIBUTION:
Found in a variety of coastal habitats on all the main islands.

USES:
None reported.

ADDITIONAL INFORMATION:
This salt-tolerant plant is also called the sea purslane.

Sida fallax
HAWAIIAN NAME: **'Ilima**
Indigenous

IDENTIFICATION:

A low-lying plant with heart-shaped 1-inch-long leaves. The yellow-orange flowers have 5 petals.

DISTRIBUTION:

This is one of the most common native species still found in Hawaiian coastal areas. Different varieties grow from sea level to 6,500 feet elevation.

USES:

About 1,000 flowers are used to make a single beautiful lei. The 'ilima, in combination with other plants, was used by Hawaiians to treat thrush, asthma, constipation and to relieve the pain of childbirth. During the hot summer, this species dries up and loses its flowers.

ADDITIONAL INFORMATION:

This is the official flower of the island of O'ahu.

Solanum nelsonii
HAWAIIAN NAME: Pōpolo
Endemic

IDENTIFICATION:
A sprawling or trailing vine-like shrub up to 3-feet tall. The leaves are about 1$^1/_2$-inches long, heart-shaped, thick and covered by fine golden hairs which give this plant a brownish hue. The white flowers are cup-shaped and have 5 petals with a lavender to dark purple center.

DISTRIBUTION:
Occurs in coastal areas from sea level to 500-feet elevation. Extremely rare or extinct on Kaua'i, O'ahu, Maui and Hawai'i. The only significant populations are found on Moloka'i and several of the northwestern Hawaiian Islands.

USES:
None reported.

ADDITIONAL INFORMATION:
Solanum nelsonii was first collected in 1778 by David Nelson, a British botanist on Captain Cook's third voyage to the Pacific. Pōpolo is in the tomato family.

Sporobolus virginicus
HAWAIIAN NAME: 'Aki 'aki
Indigenous

IDENTIFICATION:
A creeping perennial with stiff branching stems 3–16-inches high.

DISTRIBUTION:
Occurs on sandy coastal sites from sea level to 50-feet elevation. This species grows within the reach of ocean spray and can tolerate both salt air and hot sun.

USES:
None reported.

ADDITIONAL INFORMATION:
The scientific name is derived from two Greek words *sporos* meaning "seed" and *ballein*, "to throw," referring to this species' fruit, which swells and bursts after soaking, causing the seeds to be pushed out.

Tetramolopium rockii

THREATENED

HAWAIIAN NAME: None
Endemic

IDENTIFICATION:

Prostrate shrubs that form compact mats 3 inches or more in diameter and 2–3-inches high. The spatula-shaped leaves are yellowish-green or whitish. The daisy-like flower has a yellow center and many white petals.

DISTRIBUTION:

Found only on Moloka'i from 30–650-feet elevation growing on lithified calcareous sand dunes.

USES:

None reported

ADDITIONAL INFORMATION:

This species was listed as threatened on October 8, 2002. It is part of a genus that includes about 36 species that only occur in the Hawaiian Islands, Cook Islands and New Guinea.

Tribulus cistoides
HAWAIIAN NAME: Nohu
Indigenous

IDENTIFICATION:

A perennial herb that forms a sprawling mat close to the ground. The bright yellow flowers are 1 inch in diameter and have 5 petals. Leaves are 1½–5-inches long and have microscopic hairs, which prevent the surface of the leaf from drying out and help to reflect sunlight.

DISTRIBUTION:

Found on all the main islands from sea level to 300-feet elevation.

USES:

Hawaiians used this species for treating bladder diseases and thrush.

ADDITIONAL INFORMATION:

Also called the Puncture Vine because of the sharp spines on the seeds.

Vigna marina
HAWAIIAN NAME: **Nanea**
Indigenous

IDENTIFICATION:
Succulent, climbing perennial herbs. Leaves consist of 3 oval-shaped 2–4-inch long leaflets with smooth edges and rounded tips. The yellow pea-type flowers are $^1/_2$-inch long. Pods are 2-inches long and $^1/_2$-inch wide.

DISTRIBUTION:
Found from sea level to 400-feet elevation at the vegetation line on the sandy beaches of Kaua'i, O'ahu, Moloka'i, Maui and Hawai'i.

USES:
None reported for Hawai'i.

ADDITIONAL INFORMATION:
This species, also called the beach pea, is used in native medicine in the South Pacific.

Vitex rotundifolia
HAWAIIAN NAME: **Pōhinahina**

Indigenous

IDENTIFICATION:

An aromatic prostrate shrub that grows from 4–20-inches tall with small blue flowers. The leaves are $^3/_4$ –$2^1/_2$-inches long.

DISTRIBUTION:

A fairly common species that occurs on sandy beaches, dunes and rocky shores on all the main islands except Kahoʻolawe.

USES:

Pōhinahina was used medicinally.

ADDITIONAL INFORMATION:

This species is also native to Japan, China, Taiwan, Australia, India and Sri Lanka.

Waltheria indica
HAWAIIAN NAME: **'Uhaloa**
Indigenous

IDENTIFICATION:
A small shrub 2–6-feet tall with velvety hairs covering all parts of the plant. The oval leaves are up to 6-inches long and 2-inches wide with toothed edges and conspicuous veins. The fragrant yellow flowers grow in small clusters.

DISTRIBUTION:
Occurs in dry locations from sea level to 4,000-feet elevation on all the main islands.

USES:
Stems, leaves and the bark of the roots were pounded, strained and used as a gargle for sore throat. This remedy is still used today by many Hawaiians.

ADDITIONAL INFORMATION:
The genus *Waltheria* was named after A.F.Walther (1688–1746), a professor in Leipzig, Germany.

Wikstroemia uva-ursi
HAWAIIAN NAME: ʻĀkia
Endemic, Indigenous

IDENTIFICATION:
Densely branching shrubs
1–5-feet tall with dark gray-
ish-green leaves, small yellow
flowers and bright $\frac{1}{4}$-inch
diameter red berries.

DISTRIBUTION:
Occurs in a variety of habitats including hillsides, dry
ridges, lava flows and coastal
areas from 10–1,500-feet elevation on Kauaʻi, Oʻahu,
Molokaʻi and Maui.

USES:
None reported.

ADDITIONAL INFORMATION:
Wikstroemia is named after J.E.
Wikstrom, a Swedish botanist who
lived from 1789–1856. A close relative of this species, *W. oahuensis*,
was used to make fish poison.
Ethanol extracts of this species
have exhibited antitumor activity.

ALIEN
COASTAL
PLANT
SPECIES

As of 1999, there were 2,089 species of native and naturalized plants in the Hawaiian Islands. Of this total, 1,029 are native to Hawai'i, of which 89% are endemic and 1,060 are alien introductions. More alien plant species are growing in the islands' varied ecosystems than native. At least 86 of the alien species have become serious pests that threaten the continued existence of our native Hawaiian plants.

Introduced species usually have more aggressive growing strategies than native species, and once they become established, they can displace the native species by depriving them of space, water, light and nutrients. The alien species can also use allelopathy, a chemical process that a plant uses to keep other plants from growing too close to it.

Weeds also act as primary or alternate hosts for pests and diseases that the native species have no resistance to. Many of the worst alien weeds form large monotypic stands where no other plant species can survive. These infestations are similar to giant cancerous growths in the native ecosystems that, if left alone, continue to spread. Today fires, which were rare in Hawai'i before the arrival of people, spread easily because of the introduction of weedy grasses and other alien trees and plants, causing the loss of many native coastal plants.

Several of the species in the following section are either indigenous or alien. Botanists have dif-

fering opinions at present about *Abutilon incanum,*
Hibiscus tiliaceus and *Thespesia populnea.* I have
included them in this section as questionable alien
species because of the uncertainty about their status.
Perhaps as DNA testing and other scientific methods
become more developed, their method of arrival will
be fully determined. Several of the older established
alien species, including *Morinda citrifolia, Cordia subcordata,* and *Cocos nucifera,* were introduced by the
early Polynesian voyagers who settled in Hawai'i over
1,500 years ago.

The following species include some of the
worst weeds in Hawaiian coastal areas today:

Abutilon incanum
Asystasia gangetica
Atriplex semibaccata
Batis maritima
Casuarina equisetifolia
Chloris barbata
Cocos nucifera
Cordia subcordata
Hibiscus tiliaceus
Lantana camara
Leucaena leucocephala
Morinda citrifolia
Passiflora foetida
Pluchea indica
Portulaca oleracea
Prosopis pallida
Rhizophora mangle
Terminalia catappa
Thespesia populnea
Tournefortia argentea
Verbesina encelioides

Abutilon incanum
COMMON NAME: **Hoary abutilon**

NATIVE RANGE:
The deserts of Baja, California, Sonora, Mexico and the southwestern United States.

YEAR INTRODUCED TO HAWAI'I:
Unknown. Botanists are uncertain if this species was brought to Hawai'i by people or if it reached the islands without human assistance. It is currently listed as indigenous.

IDENTIFICATION:
A small shrub 1–2-feet tall. The leaves are heart-shaped and about 2-inches long. Flowers have pinkish-white petals with a dark red center.

DISTRIBUTION:
Occurs in dry areas on all the main islands from sea level to 750-feet elevation.

USES:
None reported.

THREAT LEVEL:
If the species is determined to be indigenous, the threat level would be non-existent.

Asystasia gangetica
COMMON NAME: Chinese violet

NATIVE RANGE:
Africa, India and the Malay Peninsula.

YEAR INTRODUCED TO HAWAI'I:
1925.

IDENTIFICATION: A rapidly growing perennial herb which grows 3–9-feet tall. Flowers have pale blue to purple petals, occasionally white.

DISTRIBUTION: Sea level to 1,000-feet on all the main islands.

USES: A garden plant.

THREAT LEVEL: High. This weedy species can smother all vegetation in the herbaceous layer and creates dense infestations.

Atriplex semibaccata
COMMON NAME: Australian saltbush

NATIVE RANGE:
Australia.

YEAR INTRODUCED TO HAWAI'I:
About 1895 as a possible forage plant for cattle.

IDENTIFICATION:
A perennial herb with reddish, prostrate stems up to 5-feet long and small red fruits.

DISTRIBUTION:
Naturalized on all the main islands from sea level to 500-feet elevation.

USES:
A forage plant.

THREAT LEVEL:
Medium. In areas where it occurs it can be very invasive.

Batis maritima
COMMON NAME: **Pickleweed**

NATIVE RANGE:
Coastal areas of tropical and subtropical America and the Galapagos Islands.

YEAR INTRODUCED TO HAWAI'I:
First observed growing in salt marshes near Honolulu in 1859.

IDENTIFICATION:
A low, smooth-stemmed shrub that grows 2–3-feet long with fleshy inch-long leaves that contain a salty juice that smells like pickles.

DISTRIBUTION:
Grows in extensive, dense, bright green patches near the shore.

USES:
In the West Indies, ashes of this species are used to manufacture soap and glass.

THREAT LEVEL:
High. This invasive weed has displaced several native Hawaiian marsh plants and has destroyed thousands of acres of Hawaiian wetland habitat that were formerly used as nesting areas by the endangered black-neck stilt.

Casuarina equisetifolia
COMMON NAME: **Common ironwood**

NATIVE RANGE:
Australia.

YEAR INTRODUCED TO HAWAI'I:
First planted on Kaua'i in 1882.

IDENTIFICATION:
Looks like a pine tree with long, slender, drooping needles. This species can grow to 150-feet high.

DISTRIBUTION:
Occurs in mostly low-elevation dry areas on all the main islands from sea level to 1,600-feet elevation.

USES:
As a windbreak, for erosion control and as a shade tree. The red wood is used for fuel, tapa beaters in Fiji, war clubs in Australia and to make beams, electric poles, fences, furniture, gates, house posts, mine props, oars, pavings, pilings, rafters, roofing shingles, tool handles, and wagon wheels.

THREAT LEVEL:
High. The lack of other plants beneath ironwood trees suggest the release of an allelopathic agent, although Neal (1965) suggested that they deplete the nutrients in the soil. Dense thickets of ironwood displace native dune and beach vegetation. Once established, it radically alters the light, temperature and soil chemistry of beach habitats as it outcompetes and displaces native plant species.

Chloris barbata
COMMON NAME: Swolle fingergrass

NATIVE RANGE:
West Indies, Central America and South America.

YEAR INTRODUCED TO HAWAI'I:
1902.

IDENTIFICATION:
A tufted annual grass that grows up to 36-inches tall.

DISTRIBUTION:
Widely naturalized in dry, disturbed areas from sea level to 1,800-feet elevation on all the main islands.

USES:
None reported.

THREAT LEVEL:
High.

Cocos nucifera
COMMON NAME: **Coconut tree, Coco palm**

NATIVE RANGE:
Unknown; possibly Malaysian.

YEAR INTRODUCED TO HAWAI'I:
Unknown. An early Polynesian introduction.

IDENTIFICATION:
Trees with slender, curved trunks up to 100-feet tall. Leaves up to 20-feet long.

DISTRIBUTION:
Primarily coastal locations on all the main islands.

USES:
This is the best known palm in the world. The coconut shell is used to make buttons, containers, lamp stands and automobile fuel. The fresh white pulp is used for food, flavoring and feed for livestock. The husks are made into brushes, rope and mats. The leaves are used to make fans, baskets and hats. The midribs were used to make brooms and to string kukui nuts for lighting their homes. Coconut oil is used in cooking and to make soap.

THREAT LEVEL:
Minimal. *Cocos nucifera* is a weed in some parts of the world naturalizing in parts of the United States and Australia. In the USA it has been considered an environmental weed displacing native species.

Cordia subcordata
HAWAIIAN NAME: Kou

NATIVE RANGE:
Malaysia.

YEAR INTRODUCED TO HAWAI'I:
Unknown. This species was an early Polynesian introduction to Hawai'i.

IDENTIFICATION:
A small- to medium-sized tree that can grow 30-feet tall with pale gray bark, a wide-spreading crown and orange, scentless flowers.

DISTRIBUTION:
Scattered in low elevation, dry coastal areas on all the main islands except Moloka'i and Kaho'olawe.

USES:
Kou was used to make calabashes, bowls and cups. The flowers were used in leis and the seeds were eaten.

THREAT LEVEL:
Minimal.

Hibiscus tiliaceus
HAWAIIAN NAME: Hau

NATIVE RANGE:
Widespread in the tropics and sub-tropics worldwide.

YEAR INTRODUCED TO HAWAI'I:
Unknown.

IDENTIFICATION:
Small trees or shrubs 30-feet tall that can develop into impassable thickets. The 2–12-inch leaves are heart-shaped. The flowers begin the day yellow, but fade to orange then red by the afternoon.

DISTRIBUTION:
Occurs mainly along streams and in other wet coastal areas from sea level to 1,000-feet elevation.

USES:
Hau bark was used to make sandals. The fibers were made into rope. The soft, light-weight wood was made into fishing floats, outrigger canoe floats and kites. The slimy sap of hau stems and flowers was used as a mild laxative. Fires were started by rubbing the pointed end of a harder wood against a grooved piece of hau wood.

THREAT LEVEL:
This species is questionably indigenous. Botanists are not certain whether it arrived in Hawai'i on its own by seed flotation or if it was brought to the islands by the early Polynesian voyagers.

Lantana camara
COMMON NAME: Lantana

NATIVE RANGE:
West Indies.

YEAR INTRODUCED TO HAWAI'I:
1858.

IDENTIFICATION:
Thorny shrubs usually 6–10-feet tall with pungent smelling 1–5-inch long leaves and small pink, red, yellow-orange flowers.

DISTRIBUTION:
In a variety of habitats from 6–3,500-feet elevation on all the main islands and Midway.

USES:
A garden plant.

THREAT LEVEL:
High. An extremely serious weed. Several hundred thousand acres of Hawai'i are infested by this harmful species. Lantana forms dense understory thickets that crowd out and inhibit

establishment of other species. Allelopathic substances are produced by shoots and roots. In 1902, 23 insect species were introduced from Mexico for its control.

Leucaena leucocephala

HAWAIIAN NAME: Koa haole

NATIVE RANGE:
Tropical America. Today it is a widespread tropical weed.

YEAR INTRODUCED TO HAWAI'I:
1837.

IDENTIFICATION:
Fast-growing, thornless shrubs or small trees 15–30-feet tall with round white flowers and long, brown seed pods.

DISTRIBUTION:
Very common in disturbed habitats from sea level to 1,100-feet elevation.

USES:
Fodder, erosion control, firewood. Seeds are strung for leis. In the West Indies, both the pods and seeds are eaten by people. Medicinally, the bark is eaten for internal pain. Seeds and young leaves contain 4% mimosine, which causes loss of hair in horses, mules, donkeys and hogs.

THREAT LEVEL:
High. This species forms dense thickets excluding all other plants and is now the dominant tree in many Hawaiian coastal areas. It is known for its drought tolerance.

Morinda citrifolia
HAWAIIAN NAME: **Noni**

NATIVE RANGE:
Southeastern Asia to Australia.

YEAR INTRODUCED TO HAWAI'I:
Unknown. Noni was an early Polynesian introduction.

IDENTIFICATION:
This species is either a shrub or small tree 10–20-feet tall. Noni has unusual looking ovoid fruits that turn yellow when ripe. Leaves are dark green, shiny and thick. Flowers are $^1/_3$-inch long with white petals. Also called Indian mulberry.

DISTRIBUTION:
Grows from sea level to 1,500-feet elevation on all the main islands except Kaho'olawe.

USES:
The inner bark of the trunk and roots were used to make yellow dye. The immature fruit was eaten during times of famine. The leaves, fruit and bark were used for medicine. Today, noni juice is highly promoted as a health supplement, especially as an anti-cancer treatment.

THREAT LEVEL:
Minimal.

Passiflora foetida
COMMON NAME: **Love-in-a-mist**

NATIVE RANGE:
Tropical America.

YEAR INTRODUCED TO HAWAI'I:
Prior to 1871.

IDENTIFICATION:
A perennial vine with three lobed leaves and unusual looking purple and white flowers. The sweetly-tart fruit is yellow-orange and has many seeds.

DISTRIBUTION:
Common on disturbed sites from sea level to 1,600-feet elevation.

USES:

The fruit is edible, but not a common food item because it contains little pulp.

THREAT LEVEL:
High. This species forms a dense ground cover, which prevents or delays the establishment of other species.

Pluchea indica
COMMON NAME: Indian fleabane

NATIVE RANGE:
Southern Asia.

YEAR INTRODUCED TO HAWAI'I:
1915.

IDENTIFICATION:
A weedy, multi-branched shrub that can grow 6-feet tall with pale green $1^{1}/_{2}$-inch-long toothed leaves. Flowers are purple or rose and located in clusters at the end of the branches.

DISTRIBUTION:
Grows in dry coastal habitats on all the main islands except Hawai'i.

USES:
For leis and flower arrangements.

THREAT LEVEL:
Medium. This plant mainly grows in lowland habitats, particularly wetlands and fishponds where it adversely affects habitat of water birds.

Portulaca oleracea
COMMON NAME: **Pigweed or Purslane**

NATIVE RANGE:
The origin of purslane is uncertain. It can be found growing wild in many areas of the world. It existed in the New World before the arrival of Columbus, and was found in Europe by the late 16th century.

YEAR INTRODUCED TO HAWAI'I:
Prior to 1871.

IDENTIFICATION:
A smooth plant that lies close to the ground with small, dull green or reddish spatula-shaped $1/2$ –1-inch-long leaves and red stems. The yellow flowers have 5 thin petals.

DISTRIBUTION:
Low elevation disturbed habitats from sea level to 3,000-feet elevation on all the main islands except Kaho'olawe.

USES:
Eaten in salads and as a medicinal plant.

THREAT LEVEL:
Medium. An invasive weed that displaces native coastal vegetation.

Prosopis pallida

COMMON NAME: # Kiawe or Mesquite

NATIVE RANGE:
Peru, Colombia and Equador.

YEAR INTRODUCED TO HAWAI'I:
Planted by Father Bachelot in 1828 at a Catholic church in Honolulu.

IDENTIFICATION:
Fairly large trees, with a wide-spreading crown, and long, slender branches that can grow 60-feet tall. Numerous flowers are pale yellowish-green and very small. The pods are 25% grape sugar. The Hawaiian name kiawe means "to sway." Some of the young trees have sharp thorns.

DISTRIBUTION:
From sea level to 2,000-feet elevation on all the main islands except Moloka'i and Ni'ihau.

USES:
The most commercially valuable introduced tree in Hawai'i. Pods are used for fodder, the wood for fuel and piles, flowers for honey and the trees for reforestation in dry areas. In the early 1900s, people supplemented their income by selling 35-pound bags of kiawe pods for 15 cents.

THREAT LEVEL:
High. Kiawe overshadows other vegetation and the deep taproots use all available water. In many coastal areas of Hawai'i, dense, impenetrable kiawe thickets have displaced all native plants.

Rhizophora mangle
COMMON NAME: **American or Red mangrove**

NATIVE RANGE:
Florida, West Indies and South America.

YEAR INTRODUCED TO HAWAI'I:
Introduced by a sugar company to Moloka'i in 1902.

IDENTIFICATION:
A smooth, many-branched tree with aerial roots that can grow 75-feet tall. The crown is rounded. Leaves are oblong-shaped, dark green with blunt tips. Flowers are yellow and have long stems.

DISTRIBUTION:
Naturalized in salt water marshes on all the main islands except Ni'ihau and Kaho'olawe.

USES:
Bark and leaves yield tannin. Wood is used for fuel, fence material and charcoal. The bark and shoots are made into dye.

THREAT LEVEL:
High. Forms impassable thickets. On O'ahu and Moloka'i, these infestations have significantly altered most brackish water ecosystems.

Terminalia catappa
COMMON NAME: **False kamani**

NATIVE RANGE:
East Indies.

YEAR INTRODUCED TO HAWAI'I:
Prior to 1871.

IDENTIFICATION:
A small to large tree that can grow to 50-feet tall. Branches are wide-spreading. Leaves are 6–12-inches long, some of which are usually brown. The green to yellow fruit is 1–2-inches long.

DISTRIBUTION:
Thrives near sandy shores on Kaua'i, O'ahu, Maui and Hawai'i.

USES:
Edible nuts and timber used to construct houses and boats.

THREAT LEVEL:
Minimal.

Thespesia populnea
HAWAIIAN NAME: **Milo**

NATIVE RANGE:
Old World tropics.

YEAR INTRODUCED TO HAWAI'I:
Unknown. This species is either indigenous or an early Polynesian introduction.

IDENTIFICATION:
An evergreen tree that can grow to 40-feet with cup-shaped yellow flowers with a red center that turn maroon by evening and have 3–5-inch-diameter heart-shaped leaves.

DISTRIBUTION:
Occurs in coastal locations from sea level to 900-feet elevation on all the main islands. Not documented for Lāna'i or Kaho'olawe.

USES:
As a shade tree. The wood is used to make poi calabashes, dishes and platters. Milo fibers were made into cordage. The fruit wall was made into a yellow-green dye.

THREAT LEVEL:
Minimal.

Tournefortia argentea
COMMON NAME: **Tree heliotrope**

NATIVE RANGE:
Madagascar, tropical Asia, tropical Australia and Polynesia.

YEAR INTRODUCED TO HAWAI'I:
1864–1865.

IDENTIFICATION:
A small, umbrella-shaped tree with a short trunk that can grow 20-feet tall with pale, furrowed bark. The large leaves are covered with silky, whitish hairs. The small white flowers are located in spikes at or near the end of branches.

DISTRIBUTION:
Common in coastal areas on all the main islands.

USES:
In India, the leaves are eaten raw. In some areas of Polynesia, the wood is used to make tool handles and canoe bailers.

THREAT LEVEL:
Minimal.

Verbesina encelioides
COMMON NAME: **Golden crown-beard**

NATIVE RANGE:
Mexico and southwestern United States.

YEAR INTRODUCED TO HAWAI'I:
Prior to 1871.

IDENTIFICATION:
An annual branching weed 1–5-feet tall with 1$\frac{1}{2}$–4-inch long heart-shaped leaves. Flowers have yellow petals and resemble a small sunflower.

DISTRIBUTION:
Common in dry, disturbed sites from sea level to 9,000-feet elevation.

USES:
None reported.

THREAT LEVEL:
High. The dominant and aggressive growth abilities of this species prevent the growth of native coastal plants.

ADDITIONAL THREATS TO HAWAI'I'S NATIVE COASTAL PLANTS

O ver millions of years Hawaiian coastal plant species attained a natural balance. Each occupied one or more particular ecological niches determined by the amount of salt spray, sunlight, surface strata, rainfall, nutrient availability, elevation and competition. It is enjoyable to imagine how beautiful the pre-human coastal plant communities once appeared, before anything or anyone walked on the islands besides flightless birds, when everything growing in Hawai'i was native.

Their precipitous and regrettable downfall began a brief 1,500 years ago when Polynesian voyagers arrived from the Marquesas Islands. The first canoes brought dogs, pigs, chickens, rats, foreign insects and seedlings of at least 30 alien plant species including coconut, banana, sweet potato and taro. The Marquesans also brought with them a knowledge of slash-and-burn agriculture, which, over the next 12 centuries, destroyed much of the virgin coastal vegetation and transformed the land into vast agricultural areas. The human population grew to at least 300,000 during the same period.

The first description we have of the coastal areas was provided by Captain Cook, who sailed off the coast of Kaua'i on the morning of January 19, 1778:

> .... *We saw no wood but what was up*
> *in the interior part of the island and a*
> *few trees about the villages; we observed*

several plantations of Plantains and sugar canes,
and places that seemed to be planted with roots....

On November 16, 1786, Captain Nathaniel Portlock described the western shore of the island of Hawai'i:

The land appears to be laid out in distinct
plantations, every one which seemed in a high
state of cultivation.

Gathering large quantities of wood for building houses, canoes, weapons and for cooking helped to drastically alter the original native coastal and lowland vegetation. Fortunately a few areas were too remote or did not have sufficient access to water and they remained relatively undisturbed by the indigenous people.

The destructive forces affecting Hawai'i's ancient coastal plant communities greatly increased with the arrival of foreigners from the outside world, starting with Captain Cook in 1778. Grazing animals, including sheep, goats, cattle, horses and deer along with European hogs, were introduced to the islands with horrific results to the native vegetation. The hoofed newcomers ate the unprepared native plant species, which evolved in a paradise without grazing animals and for the most part lacked thorns, poisons or bad taste.

The same fragile native plants were crushed by the large herds of introduced animals.

In modern times, sugarcane and pineapple production destroyed thousands of acres of near pristine coastal lowland ecosystems. As Hawai'i's population soared to over 1,200,000, hundreds of thousands of acres of coastal land have been paved or concreted over for building freeways, roads, hotels, shopping centers, schools and homes, all of which have drastically reduced the acreage where coastal plant communities could survive. In addition, thousands of people left their neighborhoods to assault the fragile native coastal plant communities in jeeps, motorcycles and all-terrain vehicles, mindless of the terrible devastation they were causing.

In a very, very short time, a mere 1,500 years, most of the coastal plant species, which took millions of years to arrive, survive, adapt and evolve into the grand assemblage they once were, are now barely surviving as depleted, scattered remnants in disjointed and threatened areas. The large number of detrimental forces that have been responsible for their thoughtless demise are continuing to harm them without much relief. Those few vestiges that remain of the once thriving species-rich coastal plant communities need to be urgently protected from the relentless onslaughts that harm them. Everyone should participate, in any way you can, to ensure these last individuals of our timeless and priceless natural heritage will live on.

Agriculture

Native Hawaiian coastal plant communities were destroyed by extensive Polynesian agricultural development beginning in approximately 500 A.D.

During the last two centuries, tens of thousands of acres of former coastal vegetation were lost when massive sugarcane and pineapple plantations were created.

As of January 2002, 1,932,862 acres of land was classified as agricultural in the State of Hawai'i, with 46,000 acres producing sugarcane and 20,000 used for growing pineapple. Most of the large plantations and smaller farms are located in the coastal zone below 1,000-feet elevation.

Fire

Native Hawaiian coastal plants evolved in ecosystems where fires were very infrequent, only caused by occasional lava flows and rare lightning strikes. As a result, they are not adapted to recurring fires and do not quickly recover following a fire.

Alien grasses and other introduced weeds add to the fuel load and greatly increase the frequency, extent and intensity of fires. Fire-adapted alien plants can reestablish in burned areas, which reduces the amount of native plants after each fire. Fires can also destroy dormant seeds.

Grazing Animals

Hawaiian native coastal plants evolved without the presence of hoofed mammals. The grazing, trampling and rooting by introduced cattle, goats, sheep, horses, deer and pigs is destroying the last populations of many species, and altering the characteristics of entire ecosystems.

Land Development

Hundreds of miles of Hawaiian coastline have been covered by pavement and concrete. Large commercial developments, with thousands of homes, shopping centers and schools, exist along the shores of Po'ipū and

Princeville, Kaua'i; Hawai'i Kai, Waikīkī, and Honolulu, O'ahu; Kā'anapali and Kīhei, Maui and Hilo and Kona, Hawai'i. The coastlines of the islands have also been covered by airports, power plants and military bases.

Almost all of the native Hawaiian coastal vegetation that once grew in these areas no longer exists.

Off-road vehicles

All across Hawai'i, irresponsible and illegal off-road vehicle (ORV) use is threatening remaining areas of native coastal vegetation. Off-road vehicles degrade coastal habitat, and carve new roads into our last preserves. Illegally created routes erode and compact soil, destroy plants, and water quality and spread invasive weeds.

Trash

Most of the 1,052 miles of coastline in the Hawaiian Islands has been severely altered during the last 1,500 years leading to great losses of native Hawaiian coastal plant habitat, species abundance and diversity. Sadly, there are only a few special places remaining where visitors can observe significant examples of once thriving native coastal plant communities.

In these important sanctuaries a person can imagine the great natural beauty of the native vegetation that once existed along our coasts. The following locations, one on each island, are the best places to see Hawaiian native coastal plants. Additional native coastal plant species are found at these locations, but they are not included in this guide due to space limitations. There are several more locations on each island where significant numbers of native coastal species remain and these can be easily

found if one does some exploring and research.

Several rare and endangered species which appear in the text have no locations mentioned for them. This is done to ensure they receive maximum protection from possible trampling or removal.

When you visit areas where native Hawaiian coastal plants grow, please stay on the trail and avoid stepping on any plants or damaging the fragile surrounding areas.

When visiting these areas be prepared for hot and dry conditions. Bring plenty of water, wear a hat and apply sunscreen. It is best to go early in the morning to avoid the heat and to get the best look at several of the species' flowers, which close by late morning.

For more information on the native plant locations mentioned in this guide please call Hawai'i State Parks Department at 808-587-0300, The Nature Conservancy of Hawai'i at 808-537-4508 or the National Park Service in Hawai'i at 808-541-2693.

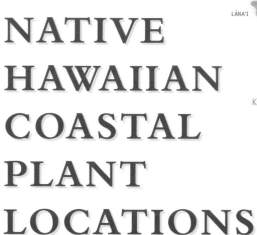

KAUA'I

Polihale

NI'IHAU

O'AHU

Ka'ena

MOLOKA'I

Mo'omomi

MAUI

LĀNA'I

KAHO'OLAWE

La Pérouse

HAWAI'I

Kaloko-Honokōhau

NATIVE HAWAIIAN COASTAL PLANT LOCATIONS

SPECIES LOCATION CHART

page #	SPECIES	Polihale	Ka'ena Point	Mo'omomi	La Perouse/Kanaio	Kaloko-Honokōhau
3	Acacia koa					
4	Achyranthes splendens		■			
5	Argemone glauca			■	■	
6	Artemisia australis	■			■	
7	Bacopa monnieri					■
8	Boerhavia repens	■				
9	Brighamia insignis					
10	Canavalia pubescens				■	
11	Capparis sandwichiana	■	■			■
12	Centaurium sebaeoides					
13	Chamaesyce celastroides	■	■			
14	Chamaesyce degeneri			■		
15	Chamaesyce skottsbergii			■		
16	Chenopodium oahuense			■		
17	Colubrina asiatica					
18	Cressa truxillensis					
19	Cuscuta sandwichiana			■		
20	Cyperus trachysanthos					
21	Diospyros sandwicensis					
22	Dodonaea viscosa	■			■	
23	Doryopteris decipiens	■		■		
24	Eragrostis variabilis					
25	Erythrina sandwicensis				■	
26	Fimbristylis cymosa	■		■	■	
27	Gossypium tomentosum		■			
29	Hedyotis littoralis					
30	Heliotropium anomalum	■				
31	Heliotropium curassavicum					
32	Heteropogon contortus	■	■			
33	Ipomoea pes–caprae				■	■
34	Jacquemontia ovalifolia	■	■	■	■	
35	Lepidium bidentatum					
36	Lipochaeta integrifolia			■		
37	Lipochaeta lobata					

page #	SPECIES (continued)	Polihale	Ka'ena Point	Mo'omomi	La Perouse/Kanaio	Kaloko-Honokōhau
38	Lycium sandwicense					
39	Lysimachia mauritiana					
40	Marsilea villosa					
41	Metrosideros polymorpha					
42	Myoporum sandwicense				■	■
43	Nama sandwicensis	■		■		
44	Nototrichium Sandwicense	■				
45	Osteomeles anthyllidifolia					
46	Pandanus tectorius				■	■
47	Plectranthus parviflorus		■	■		
48	Plumbago zeylanica		■			
49	Portalaca lutea		■	■		■
50	Portulaca molokiniensis				■	
51	Portulaca villosa			■	■	
52	Pseudognaphalium sandwicensium				■	
53	Psydrax odorata	■				
54	Reynoldsia sandwicensis					■
55	Santalum ellipticum		■			
56	Scaevola coriacea					
57	Scaevola taccada	■	■	■		■
58	Schiedea adamantis					
59	Schiedea globosa					
60	Senna gaudichaudii		■			
61	Sesbania tomentosa	■				
62	Sesuvium portulacastrum			■	■	■
63	Sida fallax		■			
64	Solanum nelsonii			■		
65	Sporobolus virginicus	■		■		
66	Tetramolopium rockii			■		
67	Tribulus cistoides		■			
68	Vigna marina					
69	Vitex rotundifolia		■			
70	Waltheria indica		■			■
71	Wikstroemia uva–ursi					
TOTAL		24	39	26	17	18

POLIHALE STATE PARK
KAUA'I

DIRECTIONS: Highway 50 from Waimea west, all the way to the end of the paved road. Continue on the dirt/sand road. The first turn on the left leads to Barking Sands Beach. If you go straight, you will come to Polihale. The state park is at the north end of the beach.

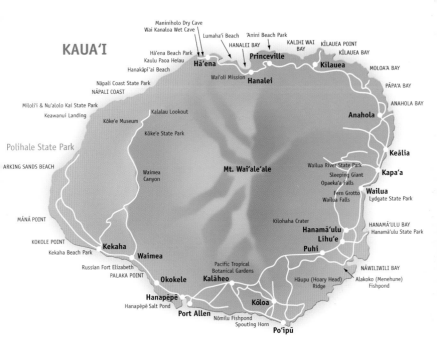

KAUA'I

Maniniholo Dry Cave
Wai Kanaloa Wet Cave
Lumaha'i Beach   'Anini Beach Park
HANALEI BAY   KALIHI WAI   KĪLAUEA POINT
                      BAY   KĪLAUEA BAY
Hā'ena Beach Park   Princeville
Kaulu Paoa Heiau   Kīlauea
Hanakāpī'ai Beach   Hā'ena   MOLOA'A BAY
                  Wai'oli Mission   Hanalei
Nāpali Coast State Park   PĀPA'A BAY
NĀPALI COAST
                                                 ANAHOLA BAY
Miloli'i & Nu'alolo Kai State Park
Keawanui Landing   Kalalau Lookout   Anahola
            Kōke'e Museum
                                                  Keālia
            Kōke'e State Park

Polihale State Park   Kapa'a
                                      Wailua River State Park
ARKING SANDS BEACH   Waimea   Mt. Wai'ale'ale   Sleeping Giant
                     Canyon   Opaeka'a Falls
                                               Fern Grotto   Wailua
                                               Wailua Falls Lydgate State Park
MĀNĀ POINT
                              Kilohaha Crater   HANAMĀ'ULU BAY
                                   Hanamā'ulu   Hanamā'ulu State Park
KOKOLE POINT   Līhu'e
Kekaha Beach Park Kekaha   Puhi
                  Waimea
                                             NĀWILIWILI BAY
Russian Fort Elizabeth   Pacific Tropical
PALAKA POINT   Botanical Gardens
          Okokele   Kalāheo   Hāupu (Hoary Head) Alakoko (Menehune)
                                   Ridge   Fishpond
          Hanapēpē   Kōloa
Hanapēpē Salt Pond
          Port Allen   Nōmilu Fishpond
                      Spouting Horn
                            Po'ipū

DESCRIPTION OF AREA: Polihale State Park encompasses nearly 140 acres of coastal lands near the westernmost point of Kaua'i. A wide sand beach backed by tall dunes in the park contain a good variety of native Hawaiian coastal plant species.

KA'ENA STATE PARK
O'AHU

DIRECTIONS: Located on the northwest corner of O'ahu and reached from the North Shore along Farrington Highway 930 from Hale'iwa and Highway 803 from Wahiawā. Continue past Dillingham Airfield until the road ends.

110

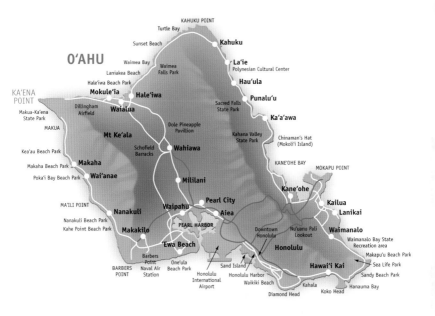

DESCRIPTION: Ka'ena Point is the westernmost tip of O'ahu. The park consists of an 853-acre strip of undeveloped coastline. A 34-acre natural area reserve is located at the end of the 2.7-mile coastal trail. The reserve includes the last relatively intact coastal dune ecosystem remaining on O'ahu and is one of the best places to see native Hawaiian coastal plant species.

Ka'ena means "the heat" and this unshaded hike can be very hot, especially during the summer. Be advised to carry several pints of drinking water, wear a hat and use sunscreen. If possible start your walk very early in the morning.

111

MOʻOMOMI NATURE CONSERVANCY PRESERVE STATE PARK
MOLOKAʻI

DIRECTIONS: Private property. The Nature Conservancy staff and volunteers lead a monthly hike through this beach dune preserve.

MOLOKA'I

DESCRIPTION: Mo'omomi Preserve contains the finest remaining examples of several Hawaiian coastal ecosystems in the state, beautiful relics from an ancient era.

For more information please contact: Moloka'i Preserves PO Box 220, Kualapu'u, HI 96757, phone: 808-553-5236, fax: 808-553-9870.

LA PÉROUSE BAY AND KANAIO STATE PARK

MAUI

DIRECTIONS: Take Makena Alanui Road south from Wailea, through Mākena. La Pérouse Bay is located at the end of the road, approximately 7 miles south of Wailea. Park near the La Pérouse historical monument. Walk along the beach until you reach a dry lava flow. Go through the fence on your left and begin walking on the "Kings Highway" through the 1790 lava flow. When you

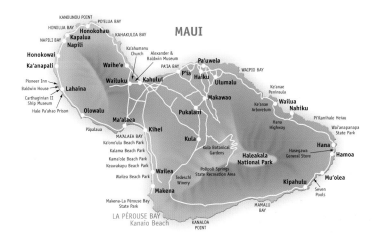

reach the "Hoapili trail" sign, you can continue straight for one mile to Kanaio Beach or take the trail to the right, which winds along the rocky coast of south La Pérouse Bay past the lighthouse and leads to several picturesque anchialine ponds.

DESCRIPTION: The arid coast south of Mākena is dominated by relatively recent lava flows that stretch up the sparse leeward slopes of Haleakalā volcano. The area is very dry and hot, especially in the summer. Excellent examples of native coastal plant communities can be seen along the jagged coast or in small areas within the extensive lava flows. Kanaio Beach is home to a good variety of native plant species.

KALOKO- HONOKŌHAU NATIONAL PARK

HAWAI'I

DIRECTIONS: Kaloko-Honokōhau is located at the base of Hualālai Volcano, along the Kona coast on the Island of Hawai'i. It is three miles north of Kailua-Kona and three miles south of Keahole-Kona International Airport, along Highway 19, the Queen Ka'ahumanu Highway.

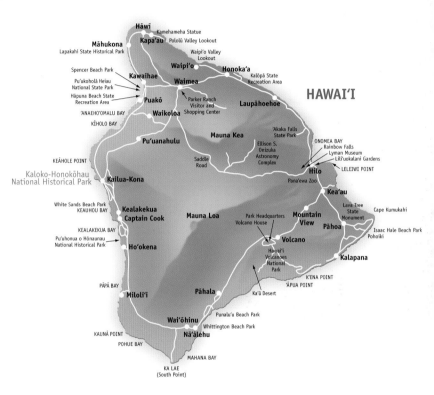

Hāwī
Kamehameha Statue
Kapaʻau Pololū Valley Lookout
Māhukona
Lapakahi State Historical Park
Waipiʻo Valley
Lookout
Spencer Beach Park   Waipiʻo
Kawaihae   Honokaʻa
Puʻukoholā Heiau   Kalōpā State
National State Park   Waimea   Recreation Area
Hāpuna Beach State   HAWAIʻI
Recreation Area   Puakō   Parker Ranch
ʻANAEHOʻOMALU BAY   Waikoloa Visitor and   Laupāhoehoe
                                Shopping Center
KĪHOLO BAY
                                ʻAkaka Falls
                Puʻuanahulu   Mauna Kea   State Park
                                                ONOMEA BAY
                                         Ellison S.   Rainbow Falls
KEĀHOLE POINT   Onizuka   Lyman Museum
                                Saddle   Astronomy   Liliʻuokalani Gardens
Kaloko-Honokōhau   Road   Complex
National Historical Park   Kailua-Kona   Hilo   LELEIWI POINT
                                                Panaʻewa Zoo
White Sands Beach Park   Keaʻau
KEAUHOU BAY   Kealakekua   Lava Tree
                Captain Cook   Mauna Loa   Park Headquarters   Mountain   State   Cape Kumukahi
                                Volcano House   View   Monument
KEALAKEKUA BAY   Pāhoa   Isaac Hale Beach Park
Puʻuhonua o Hōnaunau   Pohoiki
National Historical Park   Hoʻokena   Volcano
                                         Hawaiʻi
                                         Volcanoes   Kalapana
                                         National
PĀPĀ BAY   Park
                                                KʻENA POINT
MILOLIʻI   Miloliʻi   Pāhala   ʻĀPUA POINT
                                Kaʻū Desert
KAUNĀ POINT   Waiʻōhinu   Punaluʻu Beach Park
                Nāʻālehu   Whittington Beach Park
POHUE BAY
                MAHANA BAY
                KA LAE
                (South Point)

DESCRIPTION: The 1160-acre Kaloko-Honokōhau National Historical Park is home to at least 26 native Hawaiian plant species, 18 of which are depicted in this guide. Several species found in this hot and dry location are rare and endangered. Mostly known for its historical significance, the park is the site of an ancient Hawaiian settlement which includes portions of four different ahupuaʻa, or traditional sea to mountain land divisions.

EXTINCT NATIVE HAWAIIAN COASTAL PLANT SPECIES

IN MEMORIAM

SPECIES	Last Seen/ Collected	Location/Elevation
Achyranthes atollensis	1964	Kure Atoll/ "low sand islands"
Eragrostis mauiensis	?	Maui, Lāna'i/ "sandhills"
Haplostachys bryanii	1918	Moloka'i/ "low elevation, dry habitats"
Haplostachys munroi	1935	Lāna'i/ "West end of Lāna'i"
Kokia lanceolata	1900	O'ahu/ "Koko Head and Wailupe Valley"
Lepidium remyi	1851-1855	Hawai'i/?
Lipochaeta bryanii	?	Kaho'olawe/ ca. 984 feet
Lipochaeta degeneri	1928	Moloka'i/ "near sea level"
Lipochaeta ovata	1852	O'ahu/ "In Honolulu"
Lipochaeta perdita	1949	Ni'ihau/ "Kawaihoa Point"
Phyllostegia variabilis	1961	Kure, Midway and Laysan/ "Coastal sandy sites"
Tetramolopium conyziodes	?	Moloka'i, Maui, Lāna'i, Hawai'i/ "Coastal shrubland"
Vigna adenantha	1851-1855	O'ahu, Hawai'i/ "On Diamond Head"

Alien – Nonnative, that is, a species introduced to a place accidentally or intentionally by humans.

Allelopathy – Biochemical inhibition between higher plants, and between higher plants and soil microorganisms, resulting from the release of metabolic compounds into the soil, such as terpenes, camphor and phenolic compounds.

Annual – A plant that germinates, flowers and sets seed during a single year or growing season.

Aromatic – 1. An organic compound consisting of closed rings or carbon atoms, for example, essential oils of plants. 2. Having an aroma.

Berry – A fruit developed from a simple or compound ovary in which the ovary walls and inner tissues become enlarged and juicy, usually containing several or many seeds; more loosely, any pulpy or juicy fruit.

Biennial – A plant that completes its life cycle in two years. Flowering and fruiting usually occur only in the second year.

Calcareous – Containing lime.

Culm – The aerial stem of a grass or sedge.

Displace – To take the place of; when one species takes the place of another because of competition for resources, displacement occurs.

Dominant species – Those that control the energy flow through an ecosystem or strongly affect the environment of all other species in that ecosystem.

Drupe – A fleshy fruit arising from a single carpel and consisting of three layers: a firm exocarp; a fleshy mesocarp; and a stony or woody endocarp that encloses the solitary seed, e.g., a peach or avocado.

Ecosystem (ecological system) – The community of living organisms in a particular place, together with the non-living physical environment in which they live.

Endemic – Confined to a particular geographic area and with a specific distribution; found nowhere else.

Fern- Any of a large group of nonflowering plants having roots, stems and fronds and reproducing by spores.

Fleshy – Thick and juicy, succulent.

Fruit – The structure that develops from a ripened ovary, together with any other structures that ripen and form a unit with it. Fruits may be dry or fleshy and dehiscent or indehiscent.

Herb – A plant, either annual, biennial or perennial, with the non-woody stems dying back to the ground at the end of the growing season.

Indigenous – Belonging to the locality; not imported; native.

Infestation – To overrun in large numbers, usually so as to be harmful.

Leaf – The principal photosynthetic and transpiring organ of most plants. Leaves are usually green and basically flattened, expanded organs arising at a node as a lateral outgrowth of a stem. They usually can be subdivided into the blade and petiole. Functions may include water and food storage, protection, attachment and asexual reproduction.

Leaflets – The ultimate unit of a compound leaf.

Lobe – A projecting segment of an organ usually extending less than halfway to the base or center.

Monotypic – Containing only a single type, as a genus with only one species.

Native – An organism that originated in an area in which it lives; indigenous.

Naturalized – Thoroughly established and replacing itself by vegetative or sexual means, but originally coming from another area. As used here, introduced, intentionally or unintentionally, by man or his activities.

Ovate – Egg-shaped, with the axis widest before the middle.

Ovoid – A solid object that is ovate in outline.

Perennial – A plant that lives more than two years.

Pest – Any animal, plant or disease that is injurious to agriculture, commerce, human health or the environment.

Phyllode – An expanded, bladeless petiole that functions in photosynthesis.

Pistil – The female organ of a flower composed of one or more carpel and usually differentiated into ovary, style and stigma.

Prostrate – Flat on the ground, but not rooting at the nodes.

Rhizome – An underground stem that usually grows horizontally and, by branching or breaking, acts as a form of vegetative propagation.

Shrub – A perennial woody plant with usually several to numerous primary stems arising from or relatively near the ground. Bush.

Spine – A firm, slender, sharp-pointed structure, representing a modified leaf or stipule. A sharp, stiff projection, as on a cactus.

Succulent – Fleshy and juicy; more specifically, a plant that accumulates reserves of water in the fleshy stems or leaves, due largely to the high proportion of hydrophilic colloids in the protoplasm and cell sap.

Tree – A woody perennial that usually has a single trunk.

Weed – A plant that aggressively colonizes disturbed habitats or places where it is not wanted.

BIBLIOGRAPHY

Abbott, I.A. 1992. *La'au Hawai'i: Traditional Hawaiian Uses of Plants.* Bishop Museum Press, Honolulu, HI.

Beaglehole, J.C. 1974. *The Life of Captain James Cook.* Stanford University Press, Stanford, CA.

Carlquist, S. 1970. *Hawai'i: A Natural History.* New York: Natural History Press.

Culliney, John L., and Bruce P. Koebele. 1999. *A Native Hawaiian Garden: How to Grow and Care for Island Plants.*
University of Hawai'i Press, Honolulu, HI.

Egler, F.E. 1947. *Arid Southeast O'ahu Vegetation.* Hawai'i Ecological Monographs. 17: 383–435.

Fosberg, F.R. 1961. *Guide to Excursion III.* Tenth Pacific Congress. University of Hawai'i at Mānoa, Honolulu, Hawai'i. (See Principal Terrestrial Ecosystems, pp. 19–38 and Trip to Hanauma Bay, Koko Head and Makapu'u, Southeast O'ahu, pp. 87–93).

Johnstone, Hannah Will. 1997. *Mo'omomi, West Moloka'i: A Coastal Treasure.* University of Hawai'i at Mānoa, Sea Grant Extension Service, UNIHI-CR-96-01,
Honolulu, HI.

Kimura, B.Y., and K.M. Nagata. 1980. *Hawaii's Vanishing Flora.* Oriental Publishing Company, Honolulu, HI.

Kimura, B.Y., K.M. Nagata, and R.S. Tabata, eds. 1981. *Conserving Hawaii's Coastal Ecosystems: Proceeding.* Sea Grant Cooperative Report, University of Hawai'i, Honolulu, HI.

Kirch, Patrick Vinton. 1985. *Feathered Gods and Fishhooks.* University of Hawai'i Press, Honolulu, HI.

Krauss, Beatrice H. 1993. *Plants in Hawaiian Culture.* University of Hawai'i Press, Honolulu, HI.

Krauss, Beatrice H. 2001. *Plants in Hawaiian Medicine.* Bess Press, Honolulu, HI.

Merlin, M.D. 1977. *Hawaiian Coastal Plants and Scenic Shorelines.* Oriental Publishing Company. Honolulu, HI.

Morgan, Joseph R. 1996. *Hawai'i: A Unique Geography.* Bess Press, Honolulu, HI.

Neal, M.C. *In Gardens of Hawai'i.* B. P. Bishop Museum Special Publication 50. Bishop Museum Press, Honolulu, HI.

Nagata, K.M. & B.Y. Kimura. 1980. "Hawaiian Coastal Environments, Observations of Native Flora." *Sea Grant Quarterly,* 2 (2): 6.

Portlock, Nathaniel. 1968. *A Voyage Round the World: But More Particularly to the North-West Coast of America.* Da Capo Press, New York, NY.

Pratt, H. Douglas. 1998. *A Pocket Guide to Hawai'i's Trees and Shrubs.* Mutual Publishing, Honolulu, HI.

Richmond, T. de A., and D. Mueller-Dombois. 1972. "Coastline Ecosystems on O'ahu, Hawai'i." *Vegetation,* 25 (5–6): 367–460.

Ripperton, J.C., and E.Y. Hosaka. 1942. "Vegetation Zones of Hawaii." *Hawaii Agric. Exp. Sta Bull.* 89: 60.

Sohmer, S.H., and R. Gustafson. 1987. *Plants and Flowers of Hawai'i.* University of Hawai'i Press, Honolulu, HI.

Stone, Charles P., and Danielle B. Stone, eds. 1989. *Conservation Biology in Hawai'i.* Cooperative National Park Resources Studies Unit, University of Hawai'i at Mānoa, Honolulu, HI.

Tabata, R.S. 1979. *An Introduction to Hawaiian Coastal Plants.* U.H. Sea Grant College Program, Marine Advisory Program, UNIHI-SEAGRANT-AB-80-01, Honolulu, HI.

Tabata, R.S. 1980. "The Native Coastal Plants of O'ahu Hawai'i," *Newsletter of the Hawaiian Botanical Society*, 19: 2–44.

Valier, Kathy. 1995. *Ferns of Hawai'i.* University of Hawai'i Press, Honolulu, HI.

Wagner, W., and S.H. Somer. 1990. *Manual of the Flowering Plants of Hawai'i, Vol. I and Vol. 2.* University of Hawai'i Press and Bishop Museum Press, Honolulu, HI.

Whistler, W.A. 1980. *Coastal Flowers of the Tropical Pacific.* Tropical Botanical Garden, Lāwa'i, Kaua'i, HI.

Whistler, W.A. 1995. *Wayside Plants of the Islands: A Guide to the Lowland Flora of the Pacific Islands including Hawai'i, Samoa, Tonga, Tahiti, Fiji, Guam, Belau.* Everbest Printing Company, Ltd., Hong Kong.

Born in Cleveland, Ohio, and raised in Los Angeles, California, Michael Walther first visited Hawaiʻi in December 1972. In 1980, he moved to Kauaʻi and while living in Poʻipū Beach, he became interested in the native honey creepers that survived in the remote Alakaʻi Wilderness. He visited the swamp-like area and attempted to see the rare ʻōʻō, ʻakialoa, oʻū, ñuku puʻu, puaiohi and kāmaʻo. Unfortunately, none of these endangered species were found, but he was able to observe the beautiful ʻiʻiwi, ʻapapane, ʻamakihi, ʻanianiau and ʻelepaio.

In November 1980, Michael returned to the mainland. During his last year in college the fate of Hawaiʻi's native birds became the focal point of his research. He chose to return to Hawaiʻi, "the endangered species capital of the world," in 1994 to study the birds and do what he could to help them survive. For three months, Michael surveyed the native forest bird populations on Kauaʻi to determine their status. His results were published in the journal of the Hawaiian Audubon Society, *ʻElepaio*.

In 1995 after graduating with high honors in anthropology and environmental studies from the Univeristy of California, Santa Barbara, he arrived on Maui and went to work as a volunteer for the National Biological Survey. Michael worked on a project studying several of the rarest birds on Earth. These included the Maui ʻākepa, Maui nukupuʻu, poʻoʻuli, Maui parrotbill and the crested honeycreeper. He worked on a research team that was surveying the wild, wet and windy slopes of the world's largest dormant volcano, Haleakalā.

Michael is also a nature photographer, and by 1997 he had collected a large number of color slides about Hawaiʻi's incredibly beautiful natural treasures. He researched and wrote *Images of Natural Hawaiʻi: A Pictorial Guide of the Aloha State's Native Forest Birds and Plants*. His photographs of Hawaiʻi's rare honey creepers have also appeared in *Hawaiʻi, Aloha, and New Zealand Forest and Bird magazines*. On Oʻahu, he continued to photograph Hawaiʻi's endangered plant and bird species and studied Hawaiian geology, archaeology, mythology and history. In the fall of 1997, Michael, with the help of his brother Mark, founded Oʻahu Nature Tours. The company's slogan is "Conservation Through Education."